Making
CONNECTIONS

1

Skills and Strategies for Academic Reading

Second Edition

Teacher's Manual

Jessica Williams

CAMBRIDGE
UNIVERSITY PRESS

CAMBRIDGE
UNIVERSITY PRESS

32 Avenue of the Americas, New York, NY 10013-2473, USA

Cambridge University Press is part of the University of Cambridge.

It furthers the University's mission by disseminating knowledge in the pursuit of education, learning and research at the highest international levels of excellence.

www.cambridge.org
Information on this title: www.cambridge.org/9781107610231

First published 2011
Second edition 2013
2nd printing 2014

Printed in the United States, by Sheridan Printing Company, Inc.

A catalog record for this publication is available from the British Library.

ISBN 978-1-107-68380-8 Student's Book
ISBN 978-1-107-61023-1 Teacher's Manual

Layout services and book design: Page Designs International, Inc.
Cover design: Studio Montage

Contents

Teaching Suggestions

The *Making Connections 1* Student's Book consists of eight units, each of which is organized in the following way:

- Two Skills and Strategies sections alternate with the readings. The first precedes Readings 1 and 2, and the second precedes Reading 3. These sections introduce and practice specific skills and strategies for reading.
- The three readings are each accompanied by associated activities in reading and vocabulary development. The final reading is the longest and most challenging.
- A final section, Making Connections, provides two cohesion-building exercises.

Students at the low-intermediate level and above need to expand their vocabulary in order to prepare for academic courses. Strategies and activities to help students expand their vocabulary are therefore important features of *Making Connections 1*. The post-reading activities following each of the three readings in a unit include tasks that facilitate vocabulary expansion by focusing on 16 vocabulary items used in the reading. Additionally, tasks for vocabulary from the Academic Word List (AWL) follow the final reading. All vocabulary items are listed and defined, with an example provided, in Appendix 1 of the Student's Book (pages 260–270). In Appendix 2 of the Student's Book (pages 271–272), each key vocabulary item is indexed by the unit and the reading in which it is first used. The ❹ icon indicates vocabulary items from the AWL.

Making Connections 1 has enough material for a reading course of 50 to 70 class hours, assuming a corresponding number of hours are available for homework assignments. Completing all the Beyond the Reading activities that accompany each reading might make the course longer.

Skills, strategies, and vocabulary are recycled within a unit and in subsequent units. It is recommended, therefore, that in planning a course outline, the order of the book be followed.

Skills and Strategies

The Skills and Strategies sections introduce reading and vocabulary-building strategies that are then incorporated into the reading activities.

Rationale

Research suggests that good readers apply various strategies when they are reading a text. The Skills and Strategies sections introduce and provide practice with a variety of these reading strategies.

Description

The first Skills and Strategies section of each unit introduces vocabulary-building skills and strategies: finding the meaning of words, noticing parts of words, collocations, and phrases. The second Skills and Strategies section in each unit focuses on reading strategies: finding the topic, main ideas and supporting details, finding contrasts, causes and effects, organizing notes into timeline and outlines, and increasing reading speed.

Each Skills and Strategies section provides two to three Skill Practice activities that move students from recognition to production. More practice in each skill is provided in the While You Read section. Students then review each skill and strategy within the Skill Review section. Strategies are recycled throughout the text.

How to Use

The Skills and Strategies sections are best introduced in class, supported by the use of other materials (e.g., examples similar to those in the Examples & Explanations subsection). At the beginning of the course, each of the Skill Practice activities should be partially completed in class. Then, when you are confident that your students understand the form and content of each activity, an appropriate number of items can be assigned for homework.

Before You Read

Connecting to the Topic

Rationale

The purpose of this activity is to get students to activate background knowledge relevant to the content of the reading that follows. Effective reading occurs when readers are able to place new information within the context of information they already possess.

Description

This is the first of two activities that occur before each reading. It consists of questions for discussion with a partner.

How to Use

This activity can be introduced through short, full-class discussions. Partners or small groups can then continue the discussions.

Previewing and Predicting

Rationale

The purpose of this activity is to get students into the habit of previewing the content and organization of a text before they start reading in depth. Previewing has been shown to be a key strategy that enhances a reader's ability to understand a text on first encounter.

Description

Making Connections 1 uses different techniques for previewing texts. Students are taught to look at titles, headings, pictures, and graphic information such as charts to guess what information might appear, or to form questions that they expect a reading to answer. Each technique encourages the student to interact with the text before beginning to read for deeper understanding.

How to Use

These activities are best introduced, modeled, and practiced in class. We recommend that students first work with a partner. The primary goal of this activity is to encourage active interaction with the text.

While You Read

Rationale

Research suggests that good readers read actively by asking themselves questions and monitoring comprehension as they read. The While You Read tasks encourage students to adopt this approach. These tasks focus students' attention on the strategic nature of the reading process during their first read-through of a text. These tasks appear in the margins of the text and force students to stop and apply the strategies presented in the earlier Skills and Strategies sections. Students are thus encouraged to do what good readers do – to interact with the text while they read.

Description

While You Read boxes are in the margin of every reading, opposite some words in bold blue within a line of text. Students are directed to stop reading at the end of the sentence containing the bold blue text and to perform a strategic task designed to support effective reading.

While You Read provides practice for the skills and strategies previously introduced. It reinforces lexical skills by having students identify context clues to meaning, figure out a word's part of speech, look up challenging words in a dictionary, and recognize collocations. It provides practice in reading skills by having students identify main ideas and supporting details and understand connections between paragraphs.

How to Use

While You Read is best introduced and modeled as a classroom activity after the reading has been previewed. We recommend that you first introduce students to the concept of active reading. You can do this by reading the first reading of Unit 1 out loud. As you come to each bold blue word, stop and read the While You Read directions. Answer the question before you continue to read. Note that this technique will be new to many students, particularly those who do not read extensively in their native language. Students will find it a time-consuming process at first, but assure them that, with practice, they will gradually apply these strategies automatically and their reading speed and comprehension will increase.

At first, many of the boxes in the shorter readings can be completed during an initial in-class read-through. This will allow you to provide students with the intensive guidance, practice, and immediate feedback on their performances that they will need as they learn to apply these skills independently.

To help students focus on the reading process, it is strongly recommended that no dictionary be used during this first read-through. We also recommend that the first read-through include reading for main ideas. (See the Main Idea Check section below.)

One challenge in the While You Read activity is that students tend to make excessive use of highlighting and/or underlining. Try to help students understand that highlighting or underlining entire paragraphs, for example, is not an effective reading strategy. In fact, indiscriminate highlighting is a counterproductive activity. To avoid this, have the students follow the directions provided in the Skills and Strategies sections: highlight main ideas only, number supporting details, and underline key vocabulary.

Reading Skill Development

Main Idea Check

Rationale

Students often focus too much on the details in a reading rather than on its main ideas. The Main Idea Check activity provides an opportunity for students to focus on an understanding of the main ideas of each paragraph. It is only after students have grasped the main ideas of a reading that they can make sense of how the details fit into this larger frame of meaning.

Description

For Unit 1 and the first two readings of Unit 2, the Main Idea Check asks students to choose from four options the sentence that best expresses the main idea of the entire reading. For the remainder of the readings, the Main Idea Check has students identify the main idea of different paragraphs by matching the paragraph number to the sentence expressing its main idea.

How to Use

Before starting the Main Idea Check tasks in Unit 1, we recommend that you read Skills and Strategies 4 in Unit 2 so that you know the main idea identification strategies that will be explicitly introduced there.

For Unit 1, and Readings 1 and 2 in Unit 2, use a simple approach with which you are comfortable, without going into the issue in any great detail. It would be helpful, for example, to have students discuss why the other choices do not represent the main idea of the reading.

After you work through the strategy-based approach to main idea identification in Skills and Strategies 4, the Main Idea Check tasks may be assigned for work in class or for homework. In classes with additional writing goals, students could be asked to rewrite the sentences of the Main Idea Check tasks in their own words and then put the sentences together to form a summary of the given reading.

A Closer Look

Rationale

Having understood the main ideas in a reading, students need to achieve a more in-depth understanding of it. In this activity, therefore, students are asked to go back to the reading and read for details and to establish connections among them.

Description

Many of the questions in A Closer Look are types of questions with which students will probably be familiar (e.g., true/false and multiple choice). We recommend that early on in the text, perhaps in Unit 2, you review some common strategies in answering multiple-choice questions. You can encourage students to use the following strategies:

- Read the directions very carefully.
- Read all the possible answers before choosing the correct one.
- Eliminate the obviously incorrect answers.
- Recognize that a wrong answer may include an incorrect fact or information not in the reading.
- Recognize that all information within the answer must be true for the answer to be correct.

You should also alert students to one question type that is possibly less familiar. To encourage the synthesizing of information, a significant number of multiple-choice questions have more than one correct answer. In these questions, students are instructed as to how many answers they should choose.

How to Use

Generally, the tasks in A Closer Look lend themselves well to completion outside of class. However, we suggest that at first you give students some classroom practice in answering this section.

A useful tool for students as they complete A Closer Look tasks is Appendix 1, Key Vocabulary (pages 260–270 in the Student's Book). This appendix lists the vocabulary alphabetically within each reading, thus providing accessible and convenient support for students during these more detailed examinations of the readings. For more information on Appendix 1, see page 7 of this Teacher's Manual.

Skill Review

Rationale

Students need multiple opportunities to practice new reading and vocabulary-building skills and strategies. This is particularly important as new skills are introduced that build upon understanding of those previously taught.

Description

The Skill Review allows students to practice specific skills introduced in the Skills and Strategies sections. The content reflects the previous reading and therefore should be sufficiently familiar to enable students to focus on the skill itself.

How to Use

This is a good homework assignment. Students can then compare their work in small groups. If students encounter problems with this task, direct them back to the appropriate Skills and Strategies section. It is worth taking the time in class to really explain these tasks since they are key to academic reading.

Vocabulary Development

Definitions

Rationale

This activity provides a simple and structured way for students to take their first steps in learning the target vocabulary in each of the 24 readings.

Description

In this activity, students find a word in the reading that is similar in meaning to each of eight given definitions. This is a simple way for students to focus on target vocabulary in context without having to use bilingual dictionaries. Part-of-speech information about the target vocabulary has been provided so that students can integrate this information into the vocabulary-learning process.

How to Use

This activity is best introduced as a classroom activity. It can then be completed either in or out of class as homework.

Words in Context

Rationale

Understanding the meaning of unknown target words by perceiving the surrounding context of the word has been demonstrated to be an important skill in vocabulary acquisition. This activity helps students to see the linguistic contexts in which the target words belong.

Description

There are three types of Words in Context activities: fill-in-the-blank within sentences, fill-in-the blanks within paragraphs, and matching. All activities introduce words or phrases from the readings that have not been targeted in the preceding Definitions exercise. The key vocabulary items are presented at the beginning of the activity.

How to Use

This activity can be completed either in or out of class. Encourage students to go back to the reading and find the target words if they cannot readily answer the questions. Although these words are recycled in later readings, we encourage you to expand this practice by creating vocabulary tests focusing on these target words. Testing students on some of the vocabulary from Unit 1 while they are working on later units, for example, will help them to retain vocabulary.

Synonyms

Rationale

Students need multiple ways to learn key vocabulary. The Synonyms activity offers the chance to focus on the meaning of key words by connecting that meaning to familiar words and phrases.

Description

Each item in the activity requires students to select the correct target vocabulary word or phrase that is closest in meaning to the words in parentheses. Students then use this information to fill in the blank lines for each sentence.

How to Use

This activity is appropriate for both in and out of class work.

Word Families

Rationale

Low-intermediate–level learners need to build their academic vocabulary quickly in order to be successful in more advanced courses. Recognizing different word forms allows students to increase their receptive vocabulary quickly and efficiently. By focusing on parts of speech, this approach to vocabulary building also may help students move toward the ability to use the vocabulary in writing and speech.

Description

This activity displays related noun and verb forms in a table. The boldface word in each table is the part of speech that appears in the reading. Students are instructed to locate the words in the reading and use context clues to figure out the meanings. If the students are still unsure, you may direct them to Appendix 1 on page 260 to check the meaning of unfamiliar vocabulary. Students choose the correct word form to complete the ten fill-in-the-blank sentences.

How to Use

We recommend that you introduce this activity in class, as students may need more instruction in parts of speech. They may also need guidance in using the correct form of the word.

Academic Word List

Rationale

The Academic Word List (Coxhead, 2000) provides a corpus of the most frequently used academic words. *Making Connections 1* provides students with the opportunity to learn this vocabulary, an activity key to preparing for academic coursework in all fields of study.

Description

After the final reading, this fill-in-the-blank activity focuses on AWL vocabulary items from the two preceding readings.

How to Use

Before you begin this activity, it is important to explain the significance of general academic vocabulary. Make sure that students know AWL items are not technical, subject-specific terms but rather general words common to all academic coursework. Research has shown that students need familiarity with this vocabulary in order to understand college texts.

The Academic Word List activity provides an opportunity for students to go back to the readings and explore vocabulary if needed. This can be done out of class, but it also works well as a group activity with students discussing possible answers and referring to the readings to explain their choices. It is recommended that students learn this vocabulary by making word cards.

Beyond the Reading

Critical Thinking

Rationale

A successful college student does not merely accumulate information. Rather, that student engages in thoughtful, reflective, and independent thinking in order to make sense of a text. Critical thinking skills enable a student to evaluate what they read, make connections, ask questions, solve problems, and apply that information to new situations.

Description

Each Critical Thinking activity defines a specific critical thinking skill and then allows students to practice that skill in a context linked to the previous reading. Examples of specific skills include clarifying concepts, applying information to new situations, and offering opinions.

How to Use

Before you begin this activity, it is a good idea to discuss the difference between memorization and comprehension. Introduce critical thinking skills as an essential part of comprehension. This is particularly important as some students may come from educational systems that emphasize rote learning rather than critical thinking. The activity itself could be assigned to in-class groups, or as homework. The latter would allow a student to spend time exploring the specific critical thinking skill. Students could then compare their responses in groups.

Research

Rationale

Some teachers may want to use the readings as an opportunity for their students to undertake some research on the topics of the readings.

Description

This activity occurs after each of the 24 readings. It offers topics for students to research and discuss that are relevant to the subject of a reading.

How to Use

The research questions offer opportunities for students to tackle more challenging reading tasks as well as to pursue more personally stimulating aspects of a given topic. Some of the research requires students to do self-reflection or survey classmates to gather more data. Some require students to go online to find additional information.

Writing

Rationale

Students develop deeper understanding of a reading and become more adept in using new vocabulary if provided an opportunity to reflect and write about what they have read.

Description

This writing activity appears at the close of each reading. It allows students to use their discussion and research activity as the basis to write short paragraphs.

How to Use

The paragraphs can be produced in or outside of class. Remind students to use information from their research activity within their writing. It is also a good idea to encourage them to use new vocabulary they have learned from that unit.

Improving Your Reading Speed

Rationale

Slow reading is a common complaint of second-language learners. It is frustrating, and it impedes comprehension. While individuals will read at different rates, gradually increasing rates for all students will allow students to read more effectively and with more pleasure and confidence.

Description

This activity appears at the end of unit. Students are directed to choose one of the previous readings within the unit and time themselves as they read. They then record their time in a chart in Appendix 3 on pages 274–275. This practice provides the opportunity for students to see their reading speed improve as they practice.

How to Use

We do not recommend that teachers suggest an ideal words-per-minute reading rate for two reasons. First, students will read at different rates. Equally important, good readers vary their rate according to a text and reading purpose. Instead, focus on improving individual rates while stressing that effective reading involves both adequate speed and comprehension.

Have students read Appendix 3 before they complete this activity. This will allow them to learn and practice strategies that will improve their reading rates. It is also important that students identify personal reading habits, such as reading out loud or looking at each individual word, that slow down reading rates.

It is a good idea to complete this activity in class the first time. You might need to help students compute their words-per-minute rates and enter these in their charts. Most of all, stress that, like any skill, improving reading speed requires practice.

Making Connections

As the final review activity of each unit, two exercises give students practice in establishing within short texts the cohesion of vocabulary, structural features, and organizational patterns.

Rationale

These tasks provide students with a focused opportunity to practice reading for cohesion between sentences and short paragraphs. In addition, students get a further opportunity to review recently targeted academic vocabulary.

Description

Units 1 to 6 introduce and give students practice with strategies writers use to achieve cohesion:

- Use of pronoun and antecedent connectors
- Connectors that signal additional information
- Connectors that signal examples

- Connectors that signal contrast
- Connectors that signal cause and effect
- Connectors that signal sequence

Units 7 and 8 allow students to review and apply all six strategies. Practice begins at the sentence level and progresses to short paragraphs. Target vocabulary from the unit is recycled throughout this Making Connections section.

How to Use

This section is probably best performed in class, where fairly immediate feedback is available. Students can work individually or in pairs. Feedback may be supplied by you and/or elicited from students. You can expand this practice by presenting other jigsaw-type activities. For example, use a paragraph that has the same cohesion-building strategies.

Appendices

Appendix 1: Key Vocabulary
(pages 260–270)

Appendix 1 is the "dictionary" for *Making Connections 1*. For each reading, the target vocabulary items are listed alphabetically, defined simply and clearly, and exemplified in a sentence. The dictionary's purpose is to offer students easy access to information on the meaning and use of each word during the vocabulary learning process, especially while they are completing the Vocabulary Development activities. It can also be used during students' work on A Closer Look. Note that vocabulary from the AWL is indicated by the ❹ icon.

Appendix 2: Index to Key Vocabulary
(pages 271–272)

Appendix 2 is an index that lists each key vocabulary item by the unit and the reading in which it is first introduced, thus allowing students to locate the original dictionary entry for a vocabulary item when necessary.

Note that vocabulary from the AWL is indicated by the ❹ icon.

Appendix 3: Improving Your Reading Speed (pages 273–275)

Appendix 3 begins with a list of strategies students can employ in order to improve their reading speed. It is a good idea to discuss these strategies before students practice this skill. It also includes a chart that students will use to record their reading rates as they work through the Student's Book.

Answer Key

1 Crossing Borders

Skills and Strategies 1
Finding the Meanings of Words

Skill Practice 1 *Page 3*

2. The officials told the travelers about the dangerous **infection** – a disease or sickness in a person's body – that was spreading in South America.
3. It is important to use different **strategies**, or plans for success, when you play chess.
4. The speaker talked for 15 minutes, and then he gave his **conclusion**. It was this last part of the talk that was most exciting.
5. At international soccer matches, fights are quite **frequent**; in other words, they occur often.
6. Since we do not know how much the tickets cost, we have to **guess**, that is, give an answer that we are not sure about.
7. The man was not sure of the **value** of the painting. In other words, he was not sure how much money to pay for it.
8. Some toys are dangerous. They can seriously **injure**, or harm, the children who play with them.

Skill Practice 2 *Page 4*

2. a disease or sickness in a person's body
3. plans for success
4. the final part of something
5. occurring often
6. give an answer that we are not sure about
7. how much money to pay for something
8. harm

Reading 1
Borders on the Land, in the Ocean, and in the Air

Connecting to the Topic *Page 5*

1. A national border is where one country ends and another country begins.
2. Answers will vary.
3. Answers will vary.
4. Answers will vary.

Previewing and Predicting *Page 5*

1. National borders are where one country ends and another country begins.
2. Answers will vary.
3. Answers will vary.

While You Read *Page 5*

1. Physical borders between countries are physical features like rivers or mountains.
2. Political borders are also lines between countries like physical borders, but governments decide where these borders will be.
3. that is, take a careful look at, everyone who enters
4. the country's border with the ocean

Reading Skill Development

Main Idea Check *Page 8*
b

A Closer Look *Page 8*

1. True
2. c
3. d
4. 1 c, 2 a, 3 d, 4 b
5. a, c, d, e

Skill Review *Page 9*
A

WORD OR PHRASE	OR	THAT IS + DEFINITION IN OTHER WORDS + DEFINITION	PUNCTU-ATION	DEFINITION IN A SENTENCE THAT FOLLOWS
physical border (*n*) Par. 1				✓
political borders (*n*) Par. 2				✓
check (*v*) Par. 3		✓		
tax (*n*) Par. 3				✓
shore (*n*) Par. 4			✓	

Vocabulary Development

Definitions *Page 10*

1. physical
2. Features
3. straight
4. control
5. official
6. Resources
7. airspace
8. permission

Synonyms *Page 10*

1. checked
2. area
3. shore
4. requested
5. cross
6. freely
7. borders
8. tax

Reading 2
Walls as Borders

Connecting to the Topic *Page 12*

Answers will vary.

Previewing and Predicting *Page 12*

a, b, d, e

While You Read *Page 12*

1. these days
2. a) Keep people safe
3. a group of computers and cameras that can tell the guards when people are crossing the border
4. on one side; on the other side

Reading Skill Development

Main Idea Check *Page 15*

d

A Closer Look *Page 15*

1. a
2. False
3. a, d
4. d
5. a, d
6. 1 c; 2 c, d; 3 a; 4 b

Skill Review *Page 16*

A

1. a
2. b
3. a
4. b

B

1. the arrival of enemies
2. reason
3. different
4. were killed

Vocabulary Development

Definitions *Page 17*

1. agree
2. Fences
3. Several
4. enemies
5. recent
6. prevent
7. suddenly
8. electronic

Words in Context *Page 17*

1. guards
2. searched
3. purpose
4. invasion
5. divide
6. entrance
7. major
8. attempt

Skills and Strategies 2
Finding the Topic of a Paragraph

Skill Practice 1 *Page 20*

1. b
2. b
3. a

Skill Practice 2 *Page 21*

1. smart cards
2. passwords
3. pets and computer chips / pets and computer identification

Reading 3
Border Control

Connecting to the Topic *Page 22*

Answers will vary.

Previewing and Predicting *Page 22*

SECTION	TOPIC
II	Using fingerprints to identify people as they cross the border
III	How our grandchildren may go from country to country
II	Using eyes to identify people as they cross the border
I	Passports
I	Documents you may need to enter different countries

While You Read *Page 22*

1. ▪
2. visa
3. In other words, takes a picture of the fingerprints and saves the picture in a computer
4. the colored part of the eye
5. In other words, everyone's iris is different.
6. new forms of identification

Reading Skill Development

Main Idea Check *Page 26*

d

A Closer Look *Page 26*

1. d
2. d
3. a, b, e
4. c

5. c
6. False
7. b, c, e
8. b

Skill Review *Page 27*

1. 3
2. 7
3. 1
4. X
5. 4

6. 2
7. X
8. 5
9. X
10. 6

Vocabulary Development

Definitions *Page 28*

1. document
2. identification
3. trick
4. unique

5. twins
6. advantage
7. store
8. disappear

Words in Context *Page 28*

1. a citizens
   b tourists
   c brief
   d depends on

2. e requires
   f technology
   g examine
   h fake

Academic Word List *Page 29*

1. documents
2. resources
3. Technology
4. requires
5. unique

6. areas
7. identification
8. features
9. major
10. physical

Making Connections

Exercise 1 *Page 31*

2. Everyone is required to show some kind of identification. The guard at the entrance will ask for it.

3. All the documents are electronic. They are stored on one computer.

4. There were three attempts to guess the password. They all failed.

5. Each person's iris is unique. That is the reason irises are good forms of identification.

6. There were separate lines for visitors and citizens. This made it faster for citizens to come back into the country.

Exercise 2 *Page 32*

1. BAC
2. ABC
3. CBA

4. CAB
5. BCA

2 Names

Skills and Strategies 3
Noticing Parts of Words

Skill Practice 1 *Page 35*

2. The baby's parents **disagreed** about what to name their baby.
3. The teacher was **careless** and always called his students by the wrong names.
4. They **renamed** their store last year, but everyone still calls it by its old name.
5. The **unofficial** name of their football team is the "Green Men."
6. Their name was difficult to spell, so they decided to **simplify** it.
7. In some **African** countries, the day when you are born becomes part of your name.
8. Some **interstate** highways in the United States are named after famous people.

Skill Practice 2 *Page 36*

2. did not agree
3. without care
4. to name again
5. not official
6. to make simple
7. connected to Africa
8. between states

Reading 1
Where Does Your Name Come From?

Connecting to the Topic *Page 37*
Answers will vary.

Previewing and Predicting *Page 37*
A
a, f

B
d

While You Read *Page 37*
1. Your given name is the name you receive when you are born.
2. incorrect
3. or large groups of families
4. c) Choosing names
5. namer

Reading Skill Development

Main Idea Check *Page 40*
c

A Closer Look *Page 40*
1. False
2. a, c
3. b
4. True
5. b
6. b

Skill Review *Page 41*
A
1. Swedish
2. Korean
3. careful
4. peaceful
5. sunny
6. professional
7. lucky
8. Mexican
9. famous
10. religious

B
1. embarrassment
2. connection
3. happiness
4. singer
5. actor

Vocabulary Development

Definitions *Page 42*
1. share
2. embarrassment
3. common
4. generally
5. select
6. professional
7. leader
8. invent

Words in Context *Page 42*
1. popular
2. honor
3. origin
4. clans
5. culture
6. customs
7. lucky
8. members

Reading 2
Changing Names

Connecting to the Topic *Page 44*
Answers will vary.

Previewing and Predicting *Page 44*
a, d, e, f

While You Read *Page 44*

1. change their names when their lives change
2. simplify
3. This means it may be difficult for them to get an education, find a job, or find a place to live
4. – another name –
5. c) an adjective

Reading Skills Development

Main Idea Check *Page 47*

a

A Closer Look *Page 47*

1. True	5. True
2. b	6. b
3. a, b, e	7. a, b, d, e
4. a, c	

Skill Review *Page 48*

A

1. traditional	5. unsafe
2. helpful	6. pronunciation
3. uncommon	7. useful
4. payment	8. unpopular

B

1. helpful	5. unpopular
2. unsafe	6. pronunciation
3. payment	7. uncommon
4. useful	8. traditional

Vocabulary Development

Definitions *Page 49*

1. identity	5. ethnic
2. Immigrants	6. face
3. fit in	7. Discrimination
4. reveal	8. serious

Synonyms *Page 49*

1. couple	5. simplified
2. Boxers	6. period
3. ordinary	7. conflict
4. entire	8. childish

Skills and Strategies 4
Finding the Main Idea of a Paragraph

Skill Practice 1 *Page 52*

1. d	3. c
2. b	4. d

Skill Practice 2 *Page 53*

1. Recent research says that a name is very important in a person's life.
2. People often like to visit towns with unusual names.
3. Many small towns are named after famous places.
4. Some towns change their names to attract visitors.

Reading 3
Names in Business

Connecting to the Topic *Page 54*

Answers will vary.

Previewing and Predicting *Page 54*

SECTION	QUESTION
I	Why are names important in business?
III	How do people feel when they hear or read a company or product name?
III	How can a product's name make people want to buy it?
II	How are names connected to companies and products?

While You Read *Page 54*

1. For example, c) First letters
2. a) Choosing names
3. b) Second sentence
4. – a large animal from Africa that runs very fast.
5. c) Naming technical products
6. powerful, (c) an adjective

Main Idea Check *Page 58*

A 6	D 4
B 3	E 8
C 5	

A Closer Look *Page 58*

1. a, c	5. 1 b, 2 d, 3 a, 4 c
2. True	6. True
3. a, b, d	7. a, c, d
4. c	8. a

Skill Review *Page 59*

PARA-GRAPH NUMBER	FIRST SEN-TENCE	SECOND SEN-TENCE	LAST SEN-TENCE	WHOLE PARA-GRAPH
1				✓
2	✓			
3		✓		
4		✓		
5	✓			
6	✓			
7	✓			
8	✓			

Vocabulary Development

Definitions *Page 60*

1. Products
2. research
3. factor
4. Customers
5. emotion
6. victory
7. modern
8. successful

Word Families *Page 60*

1. response
2. advertise
3. influence
4. advice
5. consideration
6. responded
7. influence
8. advised
9. considered
10. advertisement

Academic Word List *Page 61*

1. Immigrants
2. factor
3. professional
4. researched
5. response
6. reveal
7. period
8. selected
9. ethnic
10. conflicts

Making Connections

Exercise 1 *Page 63*

2. Names often reveal a person's <u>ethnic group</u>. They sometimes also reveal a person's <u>religious group</u>.

3. One popular name for girls in Japan in the 1990s was <u>Akiko</u>. Another was <u>Tomoko</u>.

4. Some immigrants' names are often <u>difficult to spell</u>. They are also <u>difficult to pronounce</u>.

5. Some immigrants changed <u>the spelling</u> of their names. Others changed their names <u>to something completely new</u>.

6. All the girls in the family have <u>Maria</u> in their names. One daughter is <u>Maria Angela</u>. Another daughter is <u>Anna Maria</u>.

Exercise 2 *Page 64*

1. CBA
2. ABC
3. BCA
4. ABC
5. ACB

3 Food

Skills and Strategies 5
Collocations

Skill Practice 1 *Page 67*

1. b Take
   c make
   d win
2. a have
   b take
   c offer
   d meet

3. a spend
   b take
   c do
   d get
4. a take
   b makes
   c does
   d tell

Skill Practice 2 *Page 68*

1. a have a job
   b make dinner
   d have time
2. a have arguments
   b cause problems
   c save money
   d rent a house

3. a make a mess
   b solve problems
   c take turns
   d do the dishes

Reading 1
Food from the Old World and the New World

Connecting to the Topic *Page 69*

1. Answers will vary.
2.

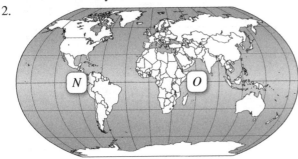

3. Answers will vary.
4. Answers will vary.

Previewing and Predicting *Page 69*
A

a, b

B

apples	O
bananas	O
beef	O
corn	N
grapes	O
oranges	O
tea	O
tomatoes	N

While You Read *Page 69*

1. eat foods from all over the world
2. raise animals, hunted animals
3. -er; (a) noun
4. foods from the New World, like chocolate and pineapples, were only for rich people

Reading Skill Development
Main Idea Check *Page 72*

A 5   D 2
B 3   E 6
C 4

A Closer Look *Page 72*

1. True
2. d
3. a, c, d
4. b
5. False
6. True
7. a N, b N, c O, d O, e N, f O, g N

Skill Review *Page 73*

A

	break-fast	dinner	food	plants	crops	ani-mals
eat	✓	✓	✓			✓
grow				✓	✓	
hunt						✓
make	✓	✓	✓			
plant					✓	
raise						✓

B

1. raise
2. grow / plant
3. grow / plant
4. raise
5. grow / plant
6. hunt

Vocabulary Development

Definitions *Page 74*

1. occur
2. explore
3. wild
4. Insects
5. exchange
6. soil
7. population
8. snack

Words in Context *Page 74*

1. a chili
   b flavor
   c crop
   d available
2. e familiar
   f rare
   g valuable
   h produce

Reading 2
Fast Food

Connecting to the Topic *Page 76*

Answers will vary.

Previewing and Predicting *Page 76*

b, c, d, f

While You Read *Page 76*

1. (a) noun, popularity
2. make money
3. Not all fast-food companies serve the same food all over the world.
4. they get heavier

Reading Skill Development

Main Idea Check *Page 79*

A 2
B 6
C 5
D 3
E 4

A Closer Look *Page 79*

1. a, b, d
2. False
3. d
4. a
5. b, d
6. c

Skill Review *Page 80*

	rice	soup	a busi-ness	5 pounds	ice cream	a kilo	salad	an of-fice
open			✓					✓
cook	✓	✓						
serve	✓	✓			✓		✓	
gain				✓		✓		

Vocabulary Development

Definitions *Page 81*

1. global
2. continent
3. majority
4. satisfy
5. effect
6. offer
7. likely
8. Consumption

Words in Context *Page 81*

1. percentage
2. gain weight
3. instead of
4. serves
5. convenient
6. tasty
7. expand
8. worry

Skills and Strategies 6
Finding Supporting Details

Skill Practice 1 *Page 84*

1. A S
   B M
2. A S
   B M
3. A S
   B M
4. A M
   B S
5. A M
   B S
6. A M
   B S

Skill Practice 2 *Page 85*

1. First, some of them are different colors.
   Second, some fruits and vegetables taste very different today.
   Finally, many fruits are much bigger today.

2. For example, in Peru, people eat gold-colored food on New Year's Day.
   In the Philippines, people eat food that is green.
   Another New Year's custom is to eat different types of beans that are shaped like coins.

3. Research shows that about half of the people in the world depend on rice for a major part of their diet.
   It takes a lot of work and a lot of water to grow rice, but one seed of rice produces about 3,000 grains of rice.
   Rice is the basis of the diet in Asia, but people grow it everywhere in the world except for Antarctica.

Reading 3
Table Manners

Connecting to the Topic *Page 86*

Answers will vary.

Previewing and Predicting *Page 86*

SECTION	QUESTION
I	What are table manners?
III	How do table manners show that we enjoy food?
III	How do people show their appreciation of food in different ways in different cultures?
I	Why are table manners important?
II	What are some examples of how table manners keep us safe?
II	What are some different ways of eating food?

While You Read *Page 86*

1. how people act at mealtimes
2. 1) long ago , people did not eat at tables. In ancient Rome, people lay down at meals.
   2) In Europe, until about 1500, there were no plates and no forks. Instead of plates, people ate their food from a piece of old, dry bread.
   3) They ate with their fingers or used pieces of bread to bring food to their mouths.
3. knives and also guns
4. One explanation for our table manners today is physical safety.

5. impolite
6. Guests who misunderstand these customs about food may eat too much, or they may go home hungry!

Reading Skill Development
Main Idea Check *Page 90*

A 9	D 6
B 7	E 8
C 2	

A Closer Look *Page 90*

1. c	5. d
2. True	6. a, b, c
3. True	7. d
4. d	

Skill Review *Page 91*

1. a The shape of knives
   b The Spanish custom that you should keep you hands visible
2. a Japanese – making noise
   b Western – finish all your food
   c Other countries – leave some food on your plate.

Vocabulary Development
Definitions *Page 92*

1. order	5. Germs
2. weapon	6. spread
3. hide	7. Hosts
4. visible	8. final

Word Families *Page 92*

1. behavior	6. behave
2. protected	7. protection
3. appreciation	8. appreciated
4. observed	9. offense
5. offended	10. observations

Academic Word List *Page 93*

1. percentage	6. global
2. majority	7. expanding
3. consumption	8. appreciation
4. final	9. available
5. visible	10. occurred

Making Connections

Exercise 1 *Page 95*

2. Today, <u>tourists can find familiar food anywhere they go</u>. For example, <u>there are many KFC restaurants in China</u>.
3. A research study in France found that <u>consumption of tea has health benefits for women</u>. For instance, <u>it may protect them from heart attacks</u>.
4. <u>We waited for 20 minutes before the waiter offered to take our order</u>. In addition, <u>he was impolite when we complained</u>.
5. <u>Shoppers can find food from all over the world in grocery stores now</u>. For example, <u>in Japan, you can buy apples from the United States and cookies from France</u>.
6. <u>The cold weather killed a large percentage of the crops</u>. In addition, <u>the price of seeds increased</u>. Farmers had a very bad year.

Exercise 2 *Page 96*

1. CAB
2. ABC
3. ACB
4. CBA
5. ABC

4 Transportation

Skills and Strategies 7
Phrases

Skill Practice 1 *Page 99*

1. a on time
   c all of a sudden
   d As a result
   e once in a while
   f In general

2. a So far
   b one by one
   c for the time being
   d At first
   e In fact
   f In the long run

Skill Practice 2 *Page 100*

1. b great deal of
   c as much as
   d day by day
   e According to
   f Meanwhile

2. a by plane
   b As a matter of fact
   c these days
   d more and more
   e instead of
   f Before too long

Reading 1
A Short History of Public Transportation

Connecting to the Topic *Page 101*

Answers will vary.

Previewing and Predicting *Page 101*

a 7
b 1
c 5
d 3

e 2
f 6
g 4

While You Read *Page 101*

1. place to place
2. Others, electric trains
3. at any time
4. Public transportation systems in other parts of the world, especially subways, have been very successful.

Reading Skill Development

Main Idea Check *Page 105*

A 2
B 6
C 5

D 4
E 3

A Closer Look *Page 105*

1. a, c
2. b
3. False
4. B → C → A → D

5. b, c
6. c
7. a 4; b 1; c 3; d 2

Skill Review *Page 106*

1. over, country
2. place, place
3. on, whole

4. at, time
5. end, of
6. and

Vocabulary Development

Definitions *Page 107*

1. crowded
2. Tunnels
3. system
4. narrow

5. wide
6. Locations
7. efficient
8. Energy

Word Families *Page 107*

1. encourage
2. pollute
3. decline
4. operation
5. pollution

6. encouragement
7. compete
8. operate
9. declined
10. competition

Reading 2
Bicycles for City Transportation

Connecting to the Topic *Page 109*

Answers will vary.

Previewing and Predicting *Page 109*

a, b, c, d, g

While You Read *Page 109*

1. They do not pollute, they are inexpensive, and they can improve health.
2. the number is increasing every year
3. all over the world
4. follow the rules
5. Bicycles also give people exercise.

Reading Skill Development

Main Idea Check *Page 113*

A 4
B 2
C 3
D 6
E 5

A Closer Look *Page 113*

1. b, c
2. True
3. c
4. b, c, d
5. d
6. b, c

Skill Review *Page 114*

1. a In 2010, there were about 200 bicycle-sharing programs in cities all over the world
   b That is almost double the number of programs in 2008.
   c Many of these programs are very successful.
2. a All bicycle riders should wear a helmet
   b They should wear something bright.
   c At night, they should always have a light on the bicycle.
3. a Riding a bicycle is less expensive than driving a car.
   b Bicycles also give people exercise.
   c They are cheaper than new buses or trains.
   d Bicycle use also reduces the number of cars, so the streets are less crowded.
   e When more people use bicycles instead of cars, air pollution decreases.

Vocabulary Development

Definitions *Page 115*

1. Traffic
2. solution
3. Rate
4. separate
5. create
6. decrease
7. helmet
8. beneficial

Words in Context *Page 115*

1. concerns
2. path
3. contrast
4. expert
5. issue
6. annual
7. significantly
8. predict

Skills and Strategies 8
Finding Contrasts

Skill Practice 1 *Page 118*

1. Starting a company is always difficult, but starting a car manufacturing company is very difficult. It requires a great deal of money and knowledge. Nevertheless, some people start new companies to build cars. Malcolm Bricklin is one of those people. He started a company in Canada to build cars in 1971. However, he did not know a lot about building cars. He had problems with the design, and it was expensive to make the cars. He sold his first cars in 1974, but the company ran out of money less than two years later. Although the company failed, the cars still win prizes at car shows.

   b It requires a great deal of money and knowledge. / Nevertheless
   c 1976 / but
   d Bricklin's cars still win prizes / although

2. Henry Ford's first car was very similar to other cars in the early 1900s. However, he tried to make his cars more cheaply. Ford's ideas about making cars were unique. First, Ford did not design cars for rich people. Instead, he wanted average people to own cars. To make his cars less expensive, he found a new way to make cars. Other car designers made cars one by one. A few workers did all the work to finish one car before they started work on the next car. At Ford's company, on the other hand, the cars moved down a line past workers. Each worker completed one part of a car as it moved down the line. In this way, Ford made more cars quickly, and sold them for less money. Ford also cared about his workers. Although other carmakers paid their workers less than $3 a day, Ford paid his workers $5 a day. He even started an English language school for his workers. Ford sold a lot of cars and became very rich, but he never forgot the people who made the cars.

   a His cars were cheaper / however
   b Average people / instead
   c The cars moved down a line past workers / on the other hand
   d No / although

Skill Practice 2 *Page 119*

When you want to buy a car, should you buy a new car or a used car? On the one hand, new cars are clean and beautiful. Old cars don't look as nice. New cars have all the newest technology. In contrast, used cars have older technology. New cars usually don't have problems, but used cars may need repairs. On the other hand, new cars are more expensive. You don't have to pay as much for a used car.

NEW CARS	USED CARS
have new technology	have older technology
don't have problems	may need repairs
are more expensive	are less expensive

Reading 3
The Dangers of Driving

Connecting to the Topic *Page 120*

Answers will vary.

Previewing and Predicting *Page 120*

SECTION	QUESTION
IV	How does technology improve car safety?
II	Does cell phone use cause accidents?
III	What are other distractions for drivers?
I	Do a lot of people die in car accidents?
IV	What can people do to make travel by car safer?
III	Is eating while driving dangerous?
II	How do cell phones distract drivers?

While You Read *Page 120*

1. but, However
2. These are the things that can take a driver's attention away from driving
3. Instead
4. Scientists and engineers are finding ways to improve safety and decrease the number of accidents.

Reading Skill Development

Main Idea Check *Page 124*

A 6
B 9
C 3
D 5
E 2

A Closer Look *Page 124*

1. True
2. b
3. d
4. False
5. True
6. a, b, e
7. c
8. b, d, e
9. b

Skill Review *Page 125*
A

1. but
2. However
3. However
4. Instead
5. Nevertheless

Vocabulary Development

Definitions *Page 126*

1. Seat belts
2. distraction
3. Passengers
4. Teenagers
5. recommend
6. shave
7. Makeup
8. Brakes

Synonyms *Page 126*

1. obeyed
2. conversation
3. estimated
4. injuries
5. avoid
6. banned
7. lead to
8. missed

Academic Word List *Page 127*

1. experts
2. create
3. annual
4. location
5. beneficial
6. significantly
7. decline
8. estimated
9. issues
10. injuries

Making Connections

Exercise 1 *Page 129*

2. In many countries all over the world, teenagers can start to drive at 18. However, in some countries, for example in New Zealand, they can get their driver's license at 15. On the other hand, in other locations, teenagers cannot drive by themselves for the first year of their license.

3. Many places have special rules for teenage drivers. For example, the rules may require teenager drivers to have an older driver in the car, or they may limit the number of passengers in the car. Teenagers may not like these rules. Nevertheless, these rules help to make the roads safe for all drivers.

4.   Motorcycles are more energy efficient than cars. Research shows that motorcycles use half the fuel that cars use. On the other hand, they are also more dangerous. Eighty percent of motorcycle accidents result in injury or death. In contrast, only 20 percent of automobile accidents result in injury or death.

5.   At one time, Los Angeles had a fast and efficient public transportation system. However, the city took away the streetcars and built more highways. Now, Los Angeles has the worst traffic in the United States. It also has very bad pollution.

Exercise 2 *Page 130*

1. CAB
2. BCA
3. ACB
4. BAC
5. CAB

5 Sleep

Skills and Strategies 9
Finding the Meanings of Words

Skill Practice 1 *Page 133*

2. a For example
3. b However
4. c that is
5. a such as

6. b but
7. b However
8. b Although

Skill Practice 2 *Page 134*

2. b
3. a
4. a
5. a

6. b
7. b
8. a

Reading 1
The Importance of Sleep

Connecting to the Topic *Page 135*

Answers will vary.

Previewing and Predicting *Page 135*

a F
b F
c T

d F
e T
f T

While You Read *Page 135*

1. (1) sleep restores your energy and helps your brain work better; (2) If you do not sleep enough, you cannot concentrate on your work; (3) Without enough sleep, you are also more likely to get sick; (4) Sleep is important for normal development.
2. There is great variation in how much they sleep
3. inactive
4. have dreams

Reading Skill Development

Main Idea Check *Page 138*

A 7
B 2
C 3

D 6
E 5
F 4

A Closer Look *Page 138*

1. False
2. d
3.

AGES	HOURS OF SLEEP
Babies	*about 16 hours*
Teenagers	*9*
Adults	*8*
People over 70 years old	*About 6 hours*

4. c
5. b
6. True

Skill Review *Page 139*

A

1. E in order to grow up strong and healthy
2. C teenagers
3. E some big snakes sleep for more than 18 hours a day. Sheep only sleep for about 4 hours, and giraffes sleep less than 2 hours a day!
4. E They sleep for a few hours, and then they stay awake for a few hours.
5. C active

B

1. transportation
2. brief
3. crowded

4. advantages
5. childish

Vocabulary Development

Definitions *Page 140*

1. restore
2. normal
3. adult
4. Patterns

5. Stages
6. strange
7. Muscles
8. paralyzed

Words in Context *Page 140*

1. d
2. c
3. f
4. h

5. g
6. b
7. a
8. e

Reading 2
Getting Enough Sleep

Connecting to the Topic Page 142

Answers will vary.

Previewing and Predicting Page 142

a, d, e, g

While You Read Page 142

1. Sleep is important for our physical health. However, sleep may be even more important for our mental health.
2. make decisions
3. you respond more slowly if you have not had enough sleep
4. when they work too hard or if they are worried about something
5. take naps

Reading Skill Development

Main Idea Check Page 145

A 3	D 5
B 2	E 6
C 7	F 4

A Closer Look Page 145

1. False	5. a, b, e
2. a, c	6. a, d
3. b, d	7. b, e, f
4. False	

Skill Review Page 146

1. For example, you must stop quickly
2. a nap – a short sleep during the day
3. In other words, of sleep – just 1 hour less
4. sleep problems, or

Vocabulary Development

Definitions Page 147

1. Mental	5. essential
2. judgment	6. Stress
3. aspect	7. nap
4. realize	8. Alcohol

Words in Context Page 147

1. ability	5. unfortunate
2. sufficient	6. fell asleep
3. at least	7. consequences
4. memory	8. comfortable

Skills and Strategies 10
Finding Causes and Effects

Skill Practice 1 Page 150

1.   Some people have trouble falling asleep. One reason may be the food they eat at night. Some foods help you sleep because they create a chemical in your body called *serotonin*. Rice, pasta, and bread are good to eat at dinner, since they create serotonin, which will make you sleepy. On the other hand, foods such as ham, cheese, and chocolate create the opposite effect from serotonin. As a result, these foods will keep you awake at night.

   b   they create a chemical in your body called *serotonin*; because
   c   they create serotonin; since
   d   these foods will keep you awake at night; as a result

2.   Recent studies show that children are sleeping less than they used to. One of the causes is that young people often have cell phones or computers in their bedrooms. Instead of going to sleep, they get on the computer or on the phone. For this reason, doctors don't think it is a good idea for children to have computers, televisions, or phones in their bedrooms. Children who get less sleep are also more likely to gain weight than other children. This happens because too little sleep makes people hungrier. Children who don't get enough sleep are tired during the daytime, so they don't want to exercise.

   a   young people often have cell phones or computers in their bedrooms; one of the causes
   b   Instead of going to sleep, they get on the computer or on the phone; for this reason
   c   too little sleep makes people hungrier; because
   d   they don't want to exercise; so

Skill Practice 2 *Page 151*

Therefore, because, because

Chart 1

CAUSE	EFFECTS
newborn babies are tiny	*cannot be alone* *they sleep with their mothers or in their parents' bed*

Chart 2

CAUSES	EFFECT
mothers worry that they will roll over their babies *it's a cultural custom*	babies put in separate beds

Reading 3
Your Body Clock

Connecting to the Topic *Page 152*

Answers will vary.

Previewing and Predicting *Page 152*

SECTION	QUESTION
III	Does everyone have the same body clock?
I	What is the body clock?
III	What happens when people have different body clocks?
II	Why do blind people have problems with their body clock?
I	What situations cause problems for the body clock?
II	What happens to people who work at night?

While You Read *Page 152*

1. You may arrive at night in Paris; your body clock thinks you are still in New York
2. Some situations can cause confusion for your body clock.
3. not every body clock is the same
4. Teenagers are not very alert in the morning; the school day begins early
5. what they did at different times every day
6. in a good / bad mood.

Reading Skill Development

Main Idea Check *Page 156*

A 7   D 2
B 5   E 8
C 6

A Closer Look *Page 156*

1. c
2. b
3. c
4. a, d
5. b
6. True
7.

STATEMENT	EARLY BIRD	NIGHT OWL
They wake up early.	✓	
They have no energy at night.	✓	
They like to stay up late.		✓
They don't like to wake up in the morning.		✓
They go to bed early.	✓	

Skill Review *Page 157*

A

1. The next morning, the alarm clock rings. It wakes you up, but your body clock thinks it is the middle of the night. As a result, you probably feel exhausted.
2. Blind people have problems with their body clocks because they cannot see the light that tells their bodies to wake up.
3. When they get home, it is bright, and their body clock tells them to stay awake. As a result, they may have trouble falling asleep.
4. It was the worst nuclear accident in history. Some scientists believe that the cause was a sleepy worker who made a mistake.
5. They are not ready to learn when they get to school. For this reason, some schools now start later in the day.
6. Most people would like to change their lives to fit their body clocks. However, this is usually not possible, so most people have to adjust their body clocks to fit their jobs, their studies, and their family life.

B

1. The next morning, the alarm clock rings. It wakes you
                                                       C
   up, but your body clock thinks it is the middle of the
                                                     E
   night. As a result, you probably feel exhausted.

2. Blind people have problems with their body clocks *E* because *C* they cannot see the light that tells their bodies to wake up.

3. When they get home, it is bright, and their body clock *C* tells them to stay awake. As a result, they may have *E* trouble falling asleep.

4. It was the worst nuclear accident in history. Some *E* scientists believe that *C* the cause was a sleepy worker who made a mistake.

5. They are not ready to learn when they get to school. *C* For this reason, some schools now start later in the *E* day.

6. Most people would like to change their lives to fit their *C* body clocks. However, this is usually not possible, *E* so most people have to adjust their body clocks to fit their jobs, their studies, and their family life.

Vocabulary Development

Definitions *Page 158*

1. affect
2. exhausted
3. permanent
4. plant
5. alert
6. Habits
7. mood
8. typical

Word Families *Page 158*

1. disturb
2. alter
3. confused
4. complaints
5. disturbance
6. adjust
7. alterations
8. complained
9. confusion
10. adjustments

Academic Word List *Page 159*

1. variation
2. concentrate
3. aspects
4. adjust
5. stress
6. mental
7. normal
8. restored
9. affects
10. sufficient

Making Connections

Exercise 1 *Page 161*

2. Thomas Edison invented the lightbulb, but did he ever imagine the consequences? Before the invention *E* of the lightbulb, people went to sleep early because *C* they did not have very much they could do after dark. As a result, they got plenty of sleep. The development of electricity let people stay awake easily and comfortably.

3. When people don't get enough sleep, they can't *C* *E* *C* concentrate very well. Because of this, there are *E* sometimes terrible accidents. For example, a huge *E* ship ran into rocks in Alaska. The reason for this *C* unfortunate accident was too little sleep.

4. Everyone knows that sleep is essential. It affects memory and mood. However, many people don't realize that it is also essential for life. In one study, *C* researchers prevented rats from sleeping for 5 days. *E* As a result, the rats died.

5. Sometimes people complain when they wake up. They say that they didn't sleep all night. It is possible they were asleep part of the night, but they thought *C* they were awake the whole night. Because of this, *E* they feel tired even when they get enough sleep.

Exercise 2 *Page 162*

1. CBA
2. ACB
3. CBA
4. ABC
5. BCA

6 Music

Skills and Strategies 11
NOTICING PARTS OF WORDS

Skill Practice 1 *Page 165*

2. united
3. technician
4. vision
5. memories
6. audible
7. automatic
8. popular

Skill Practice 2 *Page 166*

2. come together as one
3. someone with special skill
4. ability to see
5. something remembered from the past
6. able to be heard
7. able to operate by itself
8. liked by many people

Reading 1
The Power of Music

Connecting to the Topic *Page 167*

Answers will vary.

Previewing and Predicting *Page 167*

a, c, e

While You Read *Page 167*

1. play a role
2. survive
3. They use music to relieve pain and stress. It can help people who have problems speaking.
4. memory
5. they often use music in their advertisements
6. Music influences our emotions in many ways.

Reading Skill Development

Main Idea Check *Page 170*

A 6
B 4
C 2
D 5
E 3
F 7

A Closer Look *Page 170*

1. True
2. d
3. a, b, d
4. b
5. B → C → A → D
6. a, b, c

Skill Review *Page 171*
A

1. auto<u>graph</u>   *self + write*
2. con<u>nect</u>ion   *join*
3. <u>mem</u>orize   *remember*
4. micro<u>phone</u>   *sound*
5. re<u>cogn</u>ize   *know*
6. re<u>viv</u>e   *live*
7. tele<u>scope</u>   *distant*
8. <u>uni</u>que   *one*

B

1. microphone
2. telescope
3. unique
4. recognize
5. connection
6. revive
7. autograph
8. memorize

Vocabulary Development

Definitions *Page 172*

1. Cells
2. survive
3. relieve
4. recognize
5. alphabet
6. Repetition
7. Department stores
8. release

Words in Context *Page 172*

1. a role
   b patients
   c instruments
   d recover
2. e rhythm
   f energetic
   g relax
   h comfort

Reading 2
Can Anyone be a Musician?

Connecting to the Topic *Page 174*

Answers will vary.

Previewing and Predicting *Page 174*

a, b, d

While You Read *Page 174*

1. play games, make music
2. mobile
3. Mobile music apps allow ordinary people without any musical education to create their own music.
4. automatically

Reading Skill Development

Main Idea Check *Page 177*

A 5	D 2
B 3	E 4
C 6	

A Closer Look *Page 177*

1. d	4. True
2. a, d	5. True
3. b	6. B → C → D → A

Skill Review *Page 178*

Long ago, people made music by singing and playing simple instruments like drums. Music was an activity for everyone, and anyone could participate. In modern times, musical instruments became more complicated, so it took a lot of time and practice to learn to play them. As a result, not many people could learn to play musical instruments. So, making music became a job for professionals. People had to pay to hear music created and produced by professionals.

2. it took a lot of time and practice to learn
3. fewer people learned to play
4. only professionals made music
5. people had to pay to hear music

Vocabulary Development

Definitions *Page 179*

1. participate	5. portable
2. industry	6. mobile
3. complicated	7. talent
4. consumer	8. access

Words in Context *Page 179*

1. distance	5. practice
2. notes	6. equipment
3. band	7. the rest
4. unlock	8. recorded

Skills and Strategies 12
Organizing Notes in Timelines

Skill Practice 1 *Page 182*

1. In the early 1970s, a German professor started work on a project to send music over telephone lines. This was the beginning of the development of MP3 music players. It took more than 20 years to develop the technology. In 1995, researchers gave the name MP3 to this technology. Three years later, the first MP3 portable music players became available in the United States and in South Korea. Ten years after that, yearly sales of MP3 players were about 300 million.

   b more than 20 years
   c 1995
   d 1998 (Three years later)
   e 2008 (Ten years after that)

2. Wolfgang Amadeus Mozart was born in 1756 in Salzburg, Austria. His father was a well-known musician and violin teacher. Mozart started writing music when he was only five years old. By 1764, he was writing symphonies (long pieces of music for many instruments). Before he died in 1791, Mozart wrote almost 1,000 pieces of music.

   a In 1756
   b five years old
   c by 1764
   d In 1791

Skill Practice 2 *Page 183*

Rock music began in the United States. It started in Memphis, Tennessee, in 1951, with the first rock and roll record, "Rocket 88." Some of the early rock and roll singers were Chuck Berry and Elvis Presley. In the 1960s, new styles of rock and roll music began with soul music from Detroit, Michigan, and surfing music from California. Things changed in 1964 when the Beatles came to the United States from England. This was the beginning of the "British Invasion," when many rock bands came from the United Kingdom. Now, rock is international, with musicians from all over the world.

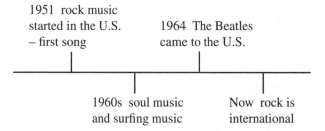

1951 rock music started in the U.S. – first song

1964 The Beatles came to the U.S.

1960s soul music and surfing music

Now rock is international

Reading 3
The Music Industry

Connecting to the Topic Page 184

Answers will vary.

Previewing and Predicting Page 184

SECTION	QUESTION
II	How did the Internet change the music business?
I	How did people listen to music before CDs?
III	What have been some recent changes in the music business?
II	Why have many people stopped downloading music?
I	When did people first begin to store music so they could listen to it any time they wanted to?
II	What is the difference between music on CDs and music on the Internet?

While You Read Page 184

1. break or scratch
2. a whole collection of songs
3. Music companies have tried many ways to stop people from sharing their music.
4. (1) they ask other companies to pay for advertisements on the music sites. (2) some music sites require customers to pay for access
5. find the best solutions

Reading Skill Development

Main Idea Check Page 188

A 4 D 2
B 8 E 6
C 3

A Closer Look Page 188

1. a, c, d
2. c
3. a, c
4. False
5. a, d
6. a N; b P; c P; d N
7. c, d

Skill Review Page 189

```
   D     E     B
 ──┼──┬──┼──┬──┼──
      A     C
```

Vocabulary Development

Definitions Page 190

1. Records
2. fragile
3. scratch
4. download
5. share
6. challenge
7. positive
8. method

Word Families Page 190

1. distribute
2. profit
3. punish
4. copy
5. distribution
6. collection
7. copy
8. collect
9. profit
10. punishment

Academic Word List Page 191

1. participates
2. equipment
3. recover
4. relax
5. access
6. positive
7. challenge
8. role
9. consumers
10. survived

Making Connections

Exercise 1 Page 193

2. In the early 1980s, CD players were very *1* expensive. After a few years, the price *2* dropped.

3. The rhythm of the music was slow *1* at first. Then the music got much faster, *2* and people started to dance.

4. In the 1950s, people could buy the *2* first portable radios. Before that, people could *1* only listen to large radios that were very heavy.

5. The website requires you to pay money. *1* Then you can download the *2* music or a movie.

6. She did not have access to music lessons *1* as a child. Later, as an adult, she took *2* piano lessons.

7. Last year all of the children participated *2* in the music program. Before that, only the *1* children with a lot of talent took part.

8. The director made them do a lot of repetitions of the
   $\overset{1}{}$
   same piece. Later, they performed the piece perfectly.
   $\overset{2}{}$

Exercise 2 *Page 194*

1. BAC
2. BAC
3. CBA
4. BCA
5. ABC

7 Natural Disasters

Skills and Strategies 13
Collocations

Skill Practice 1 *Page 197*

1. b heavy
   c high
2. a high
   b severe
   c low

3. a low
   b strong
   c heavy

Skill Practice 2 *Page 198*

1. a huge number
   b complete surprise
   d heavy traffic
2. a severe flooding
   b public meeting
   c strong support
   d low risk

3. a easy access
   b rural areas
   c natural disaster
   d urban areas

Reading 1
The Dark Side of Nature

Connecting to the Topic *Page 199*

Answers will vary.

Previewing and Predicting *Page 199*

BEGINNINGS OF PARAGRAPHS	WEATHER OR EARTHQUAKES?
Violent storms bring heavy rain and strong winds. All of the rain can cause . . . (Par. 2)	W
When floods occur in the mountains, sometimes the water mixes with earth . . . (Par. 3)	W
Movement under the earth can also cause . . . (Par. 4)	E
The most severe damage is usually at the center of an earthquake, but . . . (Par. 5)	E
Although most earthquakes are caused by the natural movement of the earth, sometimes . . . (Par. 6)	E

While You Read *Page 199*

1. serious injuries, death, significant damage; *earthquakes*
2. water mixes with earth
3. a massive wall of water that hits the shore suddenly
4. sometimes human activity contributes to natural disasters

Reading Skill Development

Main Idea Check *Page 203*

A 2
B 4
C 6

D 5
E 3

A Closer Look *Page 203*

1. a W; b ME; c W; d W; e W; f ME
2. Cyclones: c, e; Hurricanes: a, b; Typhoons: d
3. False
4. b
5. True
6. a, b, d
7. False
8. c

Skill Review *Page 204*

Violent storms bring heavy rain and strong wind. So much rain can cause floods. The most serious violent storms begin over oceans. These are called *hurricanes*, *cyclones*, or *typhoons*. Their names depend on their locations. A hurricane is a massive storm in the Atlantic Ocean or the eastern Pacific Ocean. A cyclone is a severe storm that starts in the Indian Ocean or in the southwestern Pacific Ocean near Australia or Africa. A typhoon is a storm in the northwestern Pacific Ocean near Asia. In 2009, a typhoon hit Taiwan. Eighty inches (two meters) of rain fell in two days. Heavy floods destroyed bridges and roads and caused widespread damage.

Vocabulary Development

Definitions *Page 205*

1. Damage
2. massive
3. Mud
4. deadly
5. contribute to
6. mine
7. dam
8. community

Words in Context *Page 205*

1. h
2. d
3. e
4. a
5. b
6. g
7. c
8. f

Reading 2
Predicting and Preparing for Natural Disasters

Connecting to the Topic *Page 207*

Answers will vary.

Previewing and Predicting *Page 207*

PARAGRAPH	TOPIC
2	Technology and prediction of natural disasters
6	Disaster preparation
3	Animals and earthquakes
7	Education and disaster preparation
5	Government warning systems
4	Prediction of earthquakes

While You Read *Page 207*

1. massive storms
2. small movements
3. Although we cannot predict most natural disasters, it is possible to prepare for them.
4. We cannot prevent them. However, we can predict some kinds of disasters

Reading Skill Development

Main Idea Check *Page 210*

A 5
B 3
C 6
D 4
E 7

A Closer Look *Page 210*

1. False
2. a, b
3. c
4. b T; c T
5. a, b, d
6. d

Skill Review *Page 211*

2. *After* the earthquake in Kyoko in 1975, they built an [1] early warning system. [2]

3. When a massive earthquake hit Japan in 2011, there was a warning a few seconds *after* the first tremor. [2] [1]

4. A lot of bubbles appeared in the water. *Then* the water went out very far. [1] [2]

5. For example, in Haicheng, China, in February 1975, many animals began to behave strangely. [1]
   Government officials believed this was a warning that an earthquake was coming. They ordered everyone [2] to leave the city. *A few days later*, there was a strong [3] earthquake.

Vocabulary Development

Definitions *Page 212*

1. average
2. terrible
3. precise
4. shake
5. coast
6. contact
7. crucial
8. reduce

Words in Context *Page 212*

1. tremors
2. warning
3. prepares
4. bubbles
5. satellite
6. accurately
7. loss
8. signs

Skills and Strategies 14
Organizing Notes in Outlines

Skill Practice 1 *Page 215*

Possible answers.

A. Possible to prevent loss of life in earthquakes
 1. *build better roads and buildings*
 2. *teach people what to do*
 3. *stop high-speed trains*

Skill Practice 2 *Page 215*

Possible answers.

Droughts are natural disasters.
1. *affect large numbers of people*
 a. *1920, China, killed 500,000, affected 20m*
 b. *1980s, Africa, killed millions*
2. *cause severe damage*
 a. *land blows away*
 b. *people have to leave*
3. *local officials cannot take care of people*

Reading 3
A Natural Disaster from Outer Space?

Connecting to the Topic *Page 216*

Answers will vary.

Previewing and Predicting *Page 216*

SECTION	QUESTION
II	Have objects from outer space caused natural disasters in the past?
III	Will any objects from outer space hit Earth in the future?
I	Do objects fall from outer space?
III	What can we do to prevent a natural disaster from outer space?
I	How and why do objects fall to Earth from outer space?
II	What happens when objects from outer space hit Earth?

While You Read *Page 216*

1. the air and gas above Earth
2. They disappeared from Earth forever.
3. massive destruction
4. prevent a natural disaster

Reading Skill Development

Main Idea Check *Page 220*

A 3	D 4
B 9	E 5
C 7	

A Closer Look *Page 220*

1. False	5. d
2. c	6. False
3. D → A → C → B → E	7. a
4. True	8. a, b, c, d

Skill Review *Page 221*

Paragraph 5 Main Idea:

Asteroids cause destruction but this is a natural part of how life on Earth changes.
 1 *Asteroids cause death*
 2 *Some plants and animals – extinct, others develop.*
 3 *Asteroid – development of dinosaurs*

Paragraph 6 Main Idea:

NEOs can cause major damage if they hit Earth.
 1 *Tunguska explosion = atomic bomb*
 2 *80 million trees burned*
 3 The explosion was big enough to destroy a city.

Vocabulary Development

Definitions *Page 222*

1. Outer space	5. Dust
2. Gravity	6. block
3. mystery	7. Junk
4. extinct	8. project

Word Families *Page 222*

1. analyze	6. impact
2. impact	7. analysis
3. exploded	8. explosion
4. orbits	9. suggestions
5. suggests	10. orbit

Academic Word List *Page 223*

1. widespread	6. accurately
2. precise	7. contributed to
3. community	8. impact
4. project	9. crucial
5. contacts	10. analysis

Making Connections

Exercise 1 *Page 225*

2.   Tornadoes occur all over the world. (However), they occur most often in North America. Most of these occur between the Rocky Mountains and the Appalachian Mountains. (For this reason), people call this area "Tornado Alley."

3.   At one time, scientists were not able to predict when or where tornadoes would occur. Now, (however), satellite images help them predict tornados. These images (also) can show when a tornado is nearby.

4.   Emergency officials suggest the following steps to prepare for a tornado. (First), decide which room in your building will give you the most protection. (Next), buy flashlights and some emergency supplies. (Finally), when you hear a tornado warning, move away from windows to the safest area of your building.

5.   (After) a tornado hits, officials immediately go from block to block to help injured people. (They) try to contact all the residents in the area. (Later), they survey the damage and try to figure out the losses and the precise costs of the damage.

Exercise 2 *Page 226*

1. CBA   4. BCA
2. BAC   5. CAB
3. ACB

8 Leisure

Skills and Strategies 15
Phrases

Skill Practice 1 Page 230

1. b pick up
   c move out
   d figure out

2. a put away
   b show up
   c run out of
   d cut back on

Skill Practice 2 Page 230

a mixed up
b found out
d took off

e went back
f work out

Reading 1
Work and Leisure

Connecting to the Topic Page 231

Answers will vary.

Previewing and Predicting Page 231

a, b, e

While You Read Page 231

1. looking after
2. (1) workers did not need to work as many hours
   (2) workers had more money to spend
3. get around
4. as a country's economy develops, average working hours start to decrease.

Reading Skill Development

Main Idea Check Page 234

A 7
B 3
C 4

D 2
E 6

A Closer Look Page 234

1. a, d
2. False
3. b, d

4. a, b, c
5. B → D → C → A
6. True

Skill Review Page 235

1. go out
2. get around
3. go up

4. get away
5. look after
6. take off

Vocabulary Development

Definitions Page 236

1. Factories
2. opportunity
3. public
4. Picnics

5. Concerts
6. beach
7. economy
8. similar

Word Families Page 236

1. enjoy
2. transform
3. improve
4. entertainment
5. enjoyment

6. appeared
7. entertained
8. appearance
9. improvement
10. transformation

Reading 2
Leisure Activities

Connecting to the Topic Page 238

Answers will vary.

Previewing and Predicting Page 238

Answers will vary.

While You Read Page 238

1. watch television
2. play sports
3. (1) it has made it possible to play games on computers. (2) You can play be yourself or with other people (3) Internet technology also makes it possible for people who are far apart to play games together online.
4. spend 10 billion hours

Reading Skill Development

Main Idea Check *Page 241*

A 6

B 3

C 2

D 4

E 5

A Closer Look *Page 241*

1. a, c, d
2. a
3. a, b, d
4. False
5. a
6.

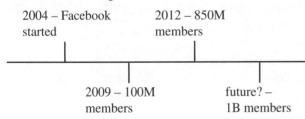

LEISURE ACTIVITY	FEATURE			
	It is productive	It requires other people	There is competition	It uses technology
Basketball		✓	✓	
Building furniture	✓			
Mahjong		✓	✓	
Online games			✓	✓
Social networks		✓		✓

Skill Review *Page 242*

2004 – Facebook started

2012 – 850M members

2009 – 100M members

future? – 1B members

Vocabulary Development

Definitions *Page 243*

1. skill
2. fix
3. Furniture
4. Games
5. Sites
6. join
7. generation
8. keep

Words in Context *Page 243*

1. productive
2. in touch
3. network
4. reached
5. united
6. apart
7. established
8. social

Skills and Strategies 16
Reading Quickly

Skill Practice 1 *Page 246*

1. b

2. a

Skill Practice 2 *Page 247*

b

Reading 3
Vacations

Connecting to the Topic *Page 248*

Answers will vary.

Previewing and Predicting *Page 248*

SECTION	QUESTION
III	Do some companies try to stop their workers from taking vacations?
I	How do most people choose to spend their vacations?
III	Why do some people keep working on their vacations?
II	What are some less traditional choices for vacations?
I	What is the history of vacations?
I	Are decisions about vacations connected to the economy?
II	Do some vacations require special knowledge?

While You Read *Page 248*

1. Vacation trends are closely related to the economy.
2. developing countries
3. find out
4. Many workers now have more time for vacations, and they have more options for their vacation time. However, a global study of workers shows that not all of them take their vacations.
5. They answer their e-mail, or they call their office to check on their work

Reading Skill Development

Main Idea Check *Page 253*

A 4

B 6

C 9

D 7

E 2

A Closer Look *Page 253*

1. a, c
2. False
3. b, c
4. a, d
5. a, b, d
6. b, c
7. a, d
8. True
9. c

Skill Review *Page 254*

Answers will vary.

Vocabulary Development

Definitions *Page 255*

1. risky
2. volunteer
3. Satisfaction
4. Assistance
5. environment
6. green
7. boss
8. employee

Words in Context *Page 255*

1. a trend
   b catch up
   c mall
   d option
2. e earn
   f put off
   g attraction
   h camping

Academic Word List *Page 256*

1. environment
2. trends
3. economy
4. similar
5. volunteers
6. established
7. options
8. transformed
9. generation
10. assistance

Making Connections

Exercise 1 *Page 258*

2. <u>Many hotels</u> around the world are trying to be green. They hope to have a smaller impact on the environment than in the past. For example, most <u>hotels</u> give <u>guests</u> an option to use their <u>towels</u> more than once before washing them.

3. The first home video game, *Pong*, appeared in 1972. People played it on their television sets. Then, when personal computers became popular, companies started to develop new games for computers. Now, home video games are very common. The Nintendo Wii, for example, is in 80 million homes.

4. Many <u>people</u> just want to relax on their vacations. Therefore, they choose vacations where they can stay home and visit local attractions. In contrast, other <u>people</u> give up their comfortable homes and go camping outdoors.

5. What is the healthiest way to spend leisure time? Most experts say that it is important to be active. In addition, communication with friends and family is also important. For these two reasons, a walk in the park together is a great way to spend free time.

Exercise 2 *Page 259*

1. BCA
2. ACB
3. BCA
4. CBA
5. ABC

Quizzes

Reading Quiz · Units 1 and 2

Read the passage. Then answer the questions that follow.

Borderlands

The areas along borders are unique because they share a history. There is often also   1
a blend of customs and traditions from the cultures on both sides of the border. One of
the longest international borders is between the United States and Mexico. The border is
more than 3,000 miles long and stretches from the south end of Texas to the California
coast. It divides two countries and two cultures.

The current border between the two countries has existed for only about 150 years.   2
During the period between 1819 and 1853, the border moved several times. Before
1819, much of the land that is now in the Western United States belonged to Mexico.
Some of the land came to the United States through agreements between the two
countries. Other areas of Mexico became part of the United States as a result of war.

The borders shifted, but most of the people and their communities did not move with   3
them. As a result, many states and cities in the southwestern part of the United States
still have the same names that they had when they were part of Mexico. California,
Nevada, Colorado, and Texas are all Spanish names. There is also a strong Mexican
influence on the culture in this area, including the music, dance, and the food people like
to eat.

Names can reveal a lot about the history of border areas. After the current border   4
between the United States and Mexico was set in the middle of the nineteenth century,
border towns grew up all along it. For more than half of its length, this border is a river.
The river has two names: It is the Rio Grande in the United States and the Rio Bravo
in Mexico. It is interesting that even on the United States' side, the name of the river
is Spanish.

From the southern tip of Texas all the way to California, there are pairs of towns and   5
cities along the border: One on the United States' side, and one on the Mexican side.
Some of them have grown so much that they almost touch and form one big city. Several
pairs of towns even have the same name on both sides; for example, Nogales and Naco
are towns that have the identical names on both sides of the border. It is also common
to have different names, but both in Spanish: El Paso and San Diego on the U.S. side
and Juarez and Tijuana on the Mexican side. Their names demonstrate that they share
history and culture, although a border now divides them.

Reading Quiz · Units 1 and 2 (continued)

A Main Idea Check

1. What is the main idea of the whole reading? (5 points)

   a. In border areas there is often a mix of cultural traditions.
   b. Names can tell us a lot about border areas.
   c. There are often conflicts between countries about the locations of borders.

2. Match each paragraph main idea below to a paragraph from the reading. Write the number of the paragraph on the blank line. (5 points)

   _____ There is a strong Mexican cultural influence north of the border.

   _____ The names of the towns along the U.S.–Mexico border show their shared history.

   _____ The location of the U.S.–Mexico border has changed throughout its history.

B A Closer Look
Look back at the reading to answer the following questions. (2 points each)

1. The U.S.–Mexican border is the longest in the world. **True or False?**

2. When was the current U.S.–Mexican border established?

   a. In 1819   b. In 1853   c. After World War II

3. Which U.S. state was *not* part of Mexico in the past?

   a. Texas   b. New Mexico   c. Florida   d. California

4. Choose the correct answers to complete the sentence.

   The aspects of Mexican culture that are found on the U.S. side of the border include _____ and _____.

   a. music   b. politics   c. food   d. religion

5. The Rio Grande and the Rio Bravo are the same river. **True or False?**

C Definitions
Find words in the reading that can complete the following definitions. (2 points each)

1. A/An _____ is a combination or mixture. (*n*) Par. 1

2. To _____ is to spread over a long distance. (*v*) Par. 1

3. To _____ means to move or change position. (*v*) Par. 3

4. If two things are _____, they are exactly the same. (*adj*) Par. 5

5. To _____ is to show something. (*v*) Par. 5

Vocabulary Quiz · Units 1 and 2

Unit 1

A The words in the box are words that you studied in Unit 1. Choose the best word to complete each sentence. You will not use all the words. (2 points each)

advantage	border	depend on	entrance	examined	fake
freely	purpose	recent	searched	stored	suddenly

1. You will need your passport when you cross the _____ into Mexico.

2. The airline's decision on whether to cancel the flight will _____ the weather forecast.

3. Terry was only 19, but he got into the club with a _____ ID that showed he was 21.

4. At the airport, an immigration official will often ask a traveler the _____ of his visit.

5. At the _____ to the walled city, there is a huge statue of the ancient king.

6. The man was stopped and _____ when he went through airport security.

7. The immigrants came from countries where they could not move around or speak

   _____ .

8. Officials carefully _____ the couple's passports and visas.

B Circle the letter of the best word to complete each sentence. The answer is always an Academic Word List word from the unit. (2 points each)

1. Everyone's fingerprints are _____ .
   a. straight   b. physical   c. brief   d. unique

2. Renting an automobile will _____ a driver's license and a credit card.
   a. require   b. attempt   c. prevent   d. check

3. The most interesting _____ of the historic city is the Presidential Palace.
   a. feature   b. invasion   c. guard   d. enemy

4. All of the man's travel _____ were in his computer case, which he'd left in the taxi.
   a. creatures   b. documents   c. tourists   d. permissions

5. When the police officer asked the man for his _____ , the man started running.
   a. request   b. resource   c. identification   d. control

6. The new immigrants settled in a/an _____ just west of the business district.
   a. shore   b. airspace   c. area   d. fence

7. A/An _____ reason that people immigrate to a new country is to find opportunities to work.
   a. straight   b. trick   c. twin   d. major

Vocabulary Quiz (continued)

Unit 2

A The words in the box are words that you studied in Unit 2. Choose the best word to complete each sentence. You will not use all the words. (2 points each)

consideration	couple	culture	fit in	generally	honor
influence	lucky	origin	popular	share	successful

1. Several of my cousins _____ the same name since they were all named after our grandfather.

2. Starbucks started as one store in Seattle in 1971 and is now _____ internationally.

3. For the past five years, Mohammed has been the most _____ baby boy's name in England and Wales.

4. Do you know the _____ of your family name?

5. In American _____, it is common to name the firstborn son after the father.

6. The name of a product can often _____ consumers' feelings about that product.

7. Younger immigrants usually find it easier than older immigrants to _____ when they arrive in a new country.

8. In some countries, a new baby's name is sometimes chosen to _____ a great leader.

B Circle the letter of the best word to complete each sentence. The answer is always an Academic Word List word from the unit. (2 points each)

1. The company is hoping that buyers will _____ positively to their new company name.
   a. face   b. respond   c. reveal   d. consider

2. Workers from North Africa who migrate to Europe often deal with a lot of _____.
   a. leaders   b. discrimination c. victory   d. members

3. When Elizabeth was offered the job, her _____ was an immediate "yes."
   a. response   b. identity   c. emotion   d. custom

4. There are several _____ one should consider before choosing between a Mac and a PC.
   a. products   b. factors   c. clans   d. advice

5. Who _____ your name: your mother or your father?
   a. simplified   b. advised   c. advertised   d. selected

6. _____ often change their names to make them easier to pronounce.
   a. Boxers   b. Professionals   c. Customers   d. Immigrants

7. Immigrant parents hope that their children will not lose their _____ identity.
   a. childish   b. modern   c. ethnic   d. ordinary

Skills and Strategies Quiz · Units 1 and 2

Unit 1

A Skills and Strategies 1: Finding the Meanings of Words
Answer the following questions about Skills and Strategies 1. (2 points each)

1. Choose the correct two words to complete the sentence.

   Writers can help readers with difficult vocabulary by using phrases such as that _____ *and in* _____ words *followed by the meaning of the word.*

   a. other   b. as   c. some   d. is

2. A good reader should look for _____ to help understand difficult vocabulary.

   a. words   b. writers   c. clues   d. bold face

3. If there is no definition immediately after a difficult word, you should check your dictionary. **True or False?**

4. Writers may use punctuation such as _____ to give a definition of a difficult word.

   a. parentheses   c. exclamation marks
   b. capital letters   d. quotation marks

5. Good readers look for words and phrases that signal a difficult word is coming up. **True or False?**

B Skills and Strategies 2: Finding the Topic of a Paragraph
Answer the following questions about Skills and Strategies 2. (2 points each)

1. Every paragraph has just one topic. **True or False?**

2. Words and phrases connected to the topic can help you _____.
   a. understand important vocabulary
   b. read more quickly
   c. understand the topic of the whole paragraph
   d. pay attention

3. You will know the topic of each paragraph in a reading if you read the first sentence of each paragraph. **True or False?**

4. The topic can be found _____.
   a. in the first sentence of a paragraph
   b. in the second sentence of a paragraph
   c. in words and phrases throughout the paragraph
   d. all of the above

5. Which question should you ask yourself in order to figure out the topic of a paragraph?
   a. What is the topic-related vocabulary in this paragraph?
   b. What does the title of the reading mean?
   c. What is this paragraph about?
   d. What is this reading about?

Skills and Strategies Quiz (continued)

Unit 2

A Skills and Strategies 3: Noticing Parts of Words

Answer the following questions about Skills and Strategies 3. (2 points each for questions 1–3; 4 points for question 4)

1. Complete the sentence with the following two words to make the statement correct.

   a. prefix   b. suffix

   When a _____ is added to a word, it creates a new word; when a _____ is added, it can tell you if a word is a noun, verb, or adjective.

2. The endings *-ous* and *-ful* tell you that a word is a/an _____.

   a. noun   b. verb   c. adjective   d. suffix

3. The suffixes *-er*, *-ist*, and *-or* all refer to a/an _____.

   a. quality or condition
   b. person or thing that does something
   c. action or process
   d. idea

4. Match each prefix to its meaning.

   1. *un-*   a. wrong
   2. *mis-*   b. again
   3. *inter-*   c. not
   4. *re-*   d. between

B Skills and Strategies 4: Finding the Main Idea of a Paragraph

Answer the following questions about Skills and Strategies 4. (2 points each)

1. The topic and the main idea of a paragraph can be in the same sentence. **True or False?**

2. If a writer asks a question at the beginning of a paragraph, _____.

   a. the question contains the main idea
   b. the answer to the question usually contains the main idea
   c. the paragraph probably will not have a main idea
   d. there probably will not be a sentence in the paragraph that contains the main idea

3. Not all paragraphs have a main idea. **True or False?**

4. Choose the correct two words to complete the sentence.

   The main _____ shows what the writer wants to say about the _____.

   a. paragraph   b. topic   c. idea   d. question

5. Look for the main idea in the paragraph you are reading because _____.

   a. it will help you understand the topic
   b. it will help you understand what the writer's purpose is
   c. it is an important reading skill
   d. all of the above

Reading Quiz · Units 3 and 4

Read the passage. Then answer the questions that follow.

Transporting Food

In 2005, a professor in the middle of the United States was having his lunch – a   1
strawberry yogurt. He estimated that everything in the yogurt – the milk, the fruit, the
sugar – had traveled more the 2,200 miles to his table. According to experts, in the
United States, most food travels for about two weeks across about 1,500 miles from
the farm to the kitchen. In addition, most U.S. meals include foods from five different
countries. The United States is not alone. Fish from Norway is shipped to China,
where it is cut into pieces and put into packages. Some of those packages travel back to
Norway. All over the world, food travels for hundreds, sometimes thousands, of miles.

Transporting food is not new. Hundreds of years ago, ships brought tea and spices   2
from Asia to Europe. They brought fruits, vegetables, and other crops back and forth
between the New World and the Old World. Today, however, significantly more food is
moving across long distances than ever before.

There are several reasons why this has happened. First, and perhaps most important,   3
is that people want all foods to be available at all times. They don't want to wait for
strawberry season to buy strawberries. Second, the systems that transport food around
the world, by land, sea, and air, have become more efficient, so it takes less time to
move products around the world. Grapes from Chile can be in a market in Germany in
just a few weeks. Third, it can be less expensive to produce or prepare food in countries
where the costs are very low. For example, it is much cheaper to cut and package the
Norwegian fish in China than it is in Norway. That is because wages are lower in China
than in Norway.

What is the effect of moving all of this food around the globe? One is that it provides   4
a rich, diverse choice of food to consumers. However, this system also has some
disadvantages. Some experts say that this system is convenient, but food that travels
long distances is not as healthy because it is not very fresh. More important, however,
all of this global transportation requires a large amount of energy. Using so much energy
can have a negative effect on the environment. For this reason, some customers prefer to
buy food from places that are nearer to their homes.

Reading Quiz · Units 3 and 4 (continued)

A Main Idea Check

1. What is the main idea of the whole reading? (5 points)

    a. The global movement of food offers consumers lots of choices but uses a lot of energy.
    b. Transporting food long distances is a good idea it makes good cheaper.
    c. Moving food all over the world is not really healthy for consumers.

2. Match each paragraph main idea below to a paragraph from the reading. Write the number of the paragraph on the blank line. (5 points)

    _____ There is a negative side to global food transportation.

    _____ Today our food moves thousands of miles before it comes to our tables.

    _____ There is a long history of transporting food around the world.

B A Closer Look
Look back at the reading to answer the following questions. (2 points each)

1. How far does most food have to travel before it arrives in U.S. homes?

    a. 2,200 miles
    b. Hundreds of thousands of miles
    c. 1,500 miles

2. What is one reason for the increase in global food transportation?

    a. Some foods no longer grow in every area so it has to be transported.
    b. Consumers want all foods to be available all the time.
    c. Energy is cheaper now than in the past.

3. The global transportation of food is a new idea. **True or False?**

4. Choose the correct answer to complete the sentence.

    Fish from Norway is sent to China for preparation and packaging because _____
    a. it is cheaper.   c. it is healthier.
    b. it is safer.   d. it saves energy.

5. Food that is produced nearby is healthier than food that has traveled a long way.
    True or False?

C Definitions
Find words in the reading that can complete the following definitions. (2 points each)

1. _____ is thick liquid food made from milk. It is often flavored with honey or fruit. (*n*) Par. 1

2. _____ are a part of a plant, for example a leaf, nut, or root, that are used to flavor food. (*n pl*) Par. 2

3. _____ are the money that workers earn. (*n pl*) Par. 3

4. If something is _____, it has a lot of variety. (*adj*) Par. 4

5. If something is _____, it is harmful or bad. (*adj*) Par. 4

Vocabulary Quiz · Units 3 and 4

Unit 3

A The words in the box are words that you studied in Unit 3. Choose the best word to complete each sentence. You will not use all the words. (2 points each)

behavior	convenient	familiar	host	likely	percentage
produces	protects	serves	valuable	wild	worries

1. Although fast food is very _____, it is also usually very unhealthy.

2. The _____ of people in developed countries who are overweight has increased sharply in the past 10 years.

3. The international aid organization _____ that food aid is not reaching the tsunami victims.

4. The dinner guests brought flowers for the _____.

5. Sara didn't know what to order from the menu since she wasn't _____ with Brazilian food.

6. The professor's _____ seemed strange, but in his culture it is common to eat with one's hands.

7. Brazil _____ coffee and sugar cane.

8. Many years ago, crops such as cocoa and pineapples were very _____.

B Circle the letter of the best word to complete each sentence. The answer is always an Academic Word List word from the unit. (2 points each)

1. She thanked the speaker and said how much the audience _____ what he had to say.
   a. offered   b. appreciated   c. spread   d. offended

2. The stars were not _____ in the cloudy night sky.
   a. visible   b. tasty   c. rare   d. final

3. The frozen yogurt business has _____ to major cities throughout the country.
   a. protected   b. expanded   c. hidden   d. observed

4. Some unhealthy foods are not _____ in schools anymore.
   a. explored   b. rare   c. available   d. final

5. In countries with high fat _____, there are higher rates of diabetes and heart disease.
   a. flavor   b. consumption   c. effect   d. crop

6. The _____ of the world's pineapples are grown in Thailand.
   a. majority   b. exchange   c. order   d. population

7. Some embarrassing situations can _____ if you don't know the mealtime customs of the people you are dining with.
   a. offer   b. observe   c. occur   d. behave

Vocabulary Quiz (continued)

Unit 4

A The words in the box are words that you studied in Unit 4. Choose the best word to complete each sentence. You will not use all the words. (2 points each)

ban	beneficial	concern	contrast	create	crowded
decrease	distraction	encourage	rate	separate	solution

1. The Tokyo subway is one of the world's busiest and most _____.

2. Texting while driving is a dangerous _____.

3. The city planners are trying to find ways to _____ the number of automobiles on the road.

4. In Rio de Janeiro, the _____ between the rich and the poor is shocking.

5. Bicycle riders want the city to _____ the bike lane from the car lane with a low wall for protection.

6. It will be difficult to find a _____ to the traffic problem in the capital city.

7. The city engineers hope to _____ a train system above the highway.

8. Television advertisements try to _____ drivers to always wear their seat belts.

B Circle the letter of the best word to complete each sentence. The answer is always an Academic Word List word from the unit. (2 points each)

1. One study _____ that 70 percent of drivers eat while they drive.
   a. creates   b. estimates   c. leads to   d. misses

2. The number of _____ deaths from bicycle accidents dropped after helmets were required.
   a. narrow   b. expert   c. annual   d. efficient

3. Texting while driving often leads to accidents causing serious _____ or even death.
   a. injury   b. energy   c. traffic   d. operation

4. As private automobile use increased, the use of public transportation _____.
   a. declined   b. obeyed   c. recommended   d. avoided

5. Cyclists asked for more bicycle lanes, saying safety was the biggest _____.
   a. path   b. conversation   c. encouragement   d. issue

6. Google Maps can help you find the _____ of the nearest bus stop.
   a. tunnel   b. location   c. system   d. brake

7. The mayor _____ that if the city builds more bicycle lanes, bicycle use will increase.
   a. competes   b. pollutes   c. predicts   d. operates

Skills and Strategies Quiz · Units 3 and 4

Unit 3

A Skills and Strategies 5: Collocations
Answer the following questions about Skills and Strategies 5. (2 points each)

1. A collocation is two or more words that often go together. **True or False?**

2. Choose the correct two words to complete the sentence.
   It is important to learn the words that go _____, not just _____ words.
   a. single   b. between   c. two   d. together

3. There can sometimes be other words that are not part of the collocation between the words of the collocation. **True or False?**

4. Knowing collocations is important because _____.
   a. good readers know these
   b. knowing them can help you read more quickly
   c. two words sometimes go together
   d. they often contain a verb and a noun

5. What is the collocation in this sentence: *She is going to make a nice hot meal.*
   a. make a meal   c. make a hot meal
   b. make a nice meal   d. make a nice hot meal

B Skills and Strategies 6: Finding Supporting Details
Answer the following questions about Skills and Strategies 6. (2 points each)

1. A well-written paragraph does not need supporting details. **True or False?**

2. Supporting details are usually _____.
   a. examples   b. facts   c. reasons   d. a, b, and c

3. Phrases such as *one explanation* and *research shows* signal to the reader that the main idea is coming next. **True or False?**

4. Choose the correct two words to complete the sentence.
   Finding supporting details will help you _____ what you _____.
   a. signal   b. read   c. understand   d. say

5. *For example* and *one reason* are examples of _____.
   a. supporting details   c. signals
   b. specific details   d. facts

Skills and Strategies Quiz (continued)

Unit 4

A Skills and Strategies 7: Phrases

Answer the following questions about Skills and Strategies 7. (2 points for questions 1–3;
4 points for question 4)

1. Fixed phrases cannot be broken up. **True or False?**

2. Fixed phrases _____.
   a. usually begin a sentence   c. are another type of collocation
   b. are rare in English   d. are not in dictionaries

3. Fixed phrases always contain three or more words. **True or False?**

4. Match each fixed phrase to its meaning.
   1. *for the time being*   a. sometimes
   2. *so far*   b. for the present time only
   3. *once in a while*   c. not late
   4. *on time*   d. until now

B Skills and Strategies 8: Finding Contrasts

Answer the following questions about Skills and Strategies 8. (2 points each)

1. A contrast can show the reader something _____.
   a. common   b. useful   c. unexpected   d. major

2. Contrast words never come in the middle of a sentence. **True or False?**

3. Choose the correct two words to complete the sentence.
   *On the _____ hand a paragraph may show contrast; on the _____ hand it can
   show similarities.*
   a. other   b. one   c. same   d. first

4. When you see a contrast word or phrase, _____.
   a. stop reading for a moment and look back at the previous sentence
   b. look for another idea in the sentence or paragraph that has a similar meaning
   c. look for the main idea of the whole paragraph
   d. find the idea in the sentence or paragraph that it is different from

5. Complete the sentence using the correct contrast signal.
   _____ *electric cars are cheaper to drive, few people buy them.*
   a. Nevertheless   b. However   c. Although   d. In contrast

Reading Quiz · Units 5 and 6

Read the passage. Then answer the questions that follow.

Music and Sleep

There is a special link between music and sleep that goes back to our childhood.   1
Most cultures have special songs that parents sing to their children to help them go to
sleep. It turns out that these *lullabies* all share specific features. They are repetitive and
slow. They have 60–80 beats per minute – very similar to the heart rate for adults. They
have a simple rhythm, and there is very little variation in the volume.

When children are young, they usually fall asleep easily. For some adults, however,   2
it is a challenge to fall asleep and stay asleep. They may not be able to relax when they
get into bed because they have a lot of stress in their daily lives. A group of doctors
wondered if lullabies could help these adults. They wanted to find out if music could
affect the quality of sleep. The doctors did an experiment with a group of scientists to
find the answer. Three groups of university students participated in the experiment. The
students had all complained that they were always exhausted because they did not sleep
well. One group listened to soft music for 45 minutes before they went to bed. The
second group listened to a recorded story. The third group did whatever they wanted
for 45 minutes before they went to bed. The first group reported that they fell asleep the
fastest and woke up the least often. The scientists also measured the breathing and heart
rates of the people in the three groups while they were sleeping. The first group had the
slowest rates, which suggested they were in a deep sleep.

Music companies have realized that this is a good business opportunity. Several   3
companies have developed special products that they say will help you fall asleep.
You can buy CDs or download this relaxing music – these lullabies for adults. The
companies claim that the music can help you fall asleep faster and more deeply, and
wake up feeling energetic. Does this really work? It is hard to say, but these products are
very popular. Some companies even sell special lullaby music for dogs. They say that
when dogs listen to the music, they will not bark. It lets them fall asleep, and as a result,
their owners can fall asleep, too!

Reading Quiz · Units 5 and 6 (continued)

A Main Idea Check

1. What is the main idea of the whole reading? (5 points)
   a. Music can reduce stress.
   b. There are many similarities in music across cultures.
   c. Music can help you fall asleep.

2. Match each paragraph main idea below to a paragraph from the reading. Write the number of the paragraph on the blank line. (5 points)

   _____ A scientific experiment showed that music can help people fall asleep.

   _____ You can buy music that may help you sleep better.

   _____ Music that helps us sleep has special features.

B A Closer Look
Look back at the reading to answer the following questions. (2 points each)

1. What is a feature that lullabies do *not* share?
   a. They are slow.   c. Their rhythm is similar to an adult heartbeat.
   b. They don't have words.   d. They have simple rhythms.

2. Adults fall asleep faster than children. **True or False?**

3. Why do many adults have trouble falling asleep?
   a. There is too much noise.
   b. They have too much stress.
   c. They eat too much food.

4. Choose the correct answers to complete the sentence.
   _____ and _____ are two signs of deep sleep.
   a. Heavy breathing   c. Slow heart rate
   b. Slow breathing   d. Dreams

5. There are lullabies that are especially for dogs. **True or False?**

C Definitions
Find words in the reading that can complete the following definitions. (2 points each)

1. A/An _____ is a connection between two things. (*n*) Par. 1

2. Something that is _____ is related to only one thing and not others. (*adj*) Par. 1

3. _____ refers to how loud a sound is. (*n*) Par. 1

4. _____ refers to how good something is. (*n*) Par. 2

5. To _____ is to make a loud, rough sound like a dog makes when it wants to communicate. (*v*) Par. 3

Vocabulary Quiz · Units 5 and 6

Unit 5

A The words in the box are words that you studied in Unit 5. Choose the best word to complete each sentence. You will not use all the words. (2 points each)

adjust	adult	breathe	disturb	essential	fall asleep
mental	nap	rapidly	realize	stress	unfortunate

1. Please don't _____ me while I'm sleeping.

2. Some people drink warm milk at bedtime to help them _____.

3. A brief 20-minute _____ during the day can refresh you for the rest of the day.

4. It can be difficult to _____ to a different time zone if you travel long distances.

5. The average _____ needs eight hours of sleep a night.

6. Reading books to their young children is a/an _____ part of their bedtime routine.

7. Sleep experts have found that _____ is a main cause of insomnia.

8. Scientists are _____ learning new and interesting things about sleep.

B Circle the letter of the best word to complete each sentence. The answer is always an Academic Word List word from the unit. (2 points each)

1. Traveling across time zones makes us _____ our sleep patterns.
   a. complain   b. restore   c. concentrate   d. alter

2. It is important to get _____ sleep and a good breakfast before an important exam.
   a. sufficient   b. alert   c. exhausted   d. at least

3. There is a lot of _____ in the number of hours different people sleep.
   a. habit   b. judgment   c. variation   d. pattern

4. Students must talk to an advisor if they need a/an _____ to their schedule.
   a. adjustment   b. complaint   c. confusion   d. development

5. The _____ of drinking coffee after dinner could be a sleepless night.
   a. stage   b. ability   c. consequence   d. memory

6. Lack of sleep can affect both your _____ and your physical health.
   a. essential   b. mental   c. typical   d. inactive

7. Getting enough sleep is an important _____ of good health.
   a. disturbance   b. dream   c. affect   d. aspect

Vocabulary Quiz (continued)

Unit 6

A The words in the box are words that you studied in Unit 6. Choose the best word to complete each sentence. You will not use all the words. (2 points each)

collection	equipment	method	notes	patient	record
repetition	rhythm	role	scratch	talent	the rest

1. The drummer travels to concerts with a lot more _____ than a guitarist does.

2. The Grammy Museum in Los Angeles has an impressive _____ of classic guitars.

3. In the past, composers wrote musical _____ by hand; now it is all done with software.

4. The first song on the singer's new album was great, but _____ of the songs were not very good.

5. My dad has an old vinyl _____ of Rolling Stones hits.

6. The Italian language is pleasing to the ear because of its beautiful _____.

7. Being a professional musician requires _____ and hard work.

8. The singer's father played an important _____ in her success.

B Circle the letter of the best word to complete each sentence. The answer is always an Academic Word List word from the unit. (2 points each)

1. After a hard day's work, it is often a good idea to _____ with a good book or soft music.
   a. challenge   b. profit   c. relieve   d. relax

2. The reaction of the fans was not very _____ when the lead guitarist threw his guitar into the crowd.
   a. positive   b. fragile   c. portable   d. complicated

3. The singer Mick Jagger is more than 70 years old, but he is still surprisingly _____.
   a. punished   b. scared   c. fragile   d. energetic

4. Many people like sing-along concerts, where everyone can _____ and sing together.
   a. practice   b. method   c. participate   d. copy

5. Fans are waiting anxiously for Lady Gaga to _____ her new album.
   a. recover   b. release   c. survive   d. collect

6. The governments of some countries do not allow _____ to Western music.
   a. access   b. consumers   c. distribution   d. equipment

7. The Internet has helped increase the _____ of music internationally.
   a. bands   b. distance   c. industry   d. distribution

Skills and Strategies Quiz · Units 5 and 6

Unit 5

A Skills and Strategies 9: Finding the Meanings of Words

Answer the following questions about Skills and Strategies 9. (6 points for question 1; 2 points each for questions 2 and 3)

1. In the following three sentences, which type of clue helps the reader find the meaning of the word *nocturnal*? Write *a*, *b*, or *c* on the blank line.

   a. definition   b. a contrast   c. an example

   _____ Nocturnal animals usually sleep during the day, but are awake throughout the night.

   _____ Owls are nocturnal animals. During the night they search for food and feed their young.

   _____ Nocturnal animals are active in the nighttime.

2. Which word in the first sentence in question 1 gives the reader a clue to the meaning of the word nocturnal?

   a. *usually*   b. *during*   c. *but*   d. *are*

3. What does *nocturnal* mean?

   a. Relating to the nighttime
   b. Relating to the daytime
   c. Relating to looking after babies and young children
   d. Relating to sleep

B Skills and Strategies 10: Finding Causes and Effects

Answer the following questions about Skills and Strategies 10. (2 points each)

1. Cause-and-effect words and phrases in a reading signal readers to look for how something happened. **True or False?**

2. Put the two words in the correct order in the following sentence.

   a. cause   b. effect

   A/an _____ happens first; a/an _____ happens next.

3. The following words or phrases signal the cause of an event. **True or False?**

   so
   therefore
   as a result

4. Another word for *effect* is _____.

   a. reason   c. beginning
   b. supporting detail   d. result

5. In the following example, the second sentence shows the effect of the event in the first sentence. **True or False?**

   He was awake all night. Because of this, he slept all day.

Skills and Strategies Quiz (continued)

Unit 6

A Skills and Strategies 11: Noticing Parts of Words
Answer the following questions about Skills and Strategies 11. (2 points each for questions 1–3; 4 points for question 4)

1. The root of a word is the basic part of a word. **True or False?**

2. From which language or languages do most roots of words in English come?
   a. French and Spanish   c. Greek and Latin
   b. German   d. Arabic

3. If you don't know the meaning of the root of a word, the first thing to do would be to _____.
   a. think of other words you know with the same root
   b. check your dictionary
   c. check the prefix or suffix
   d. read the rest of the sentence

4. Match each root to its meaning.
   1. *cogn*   a. carry
   2. *nect*   b. know
   3. *port*   c. join
   4. *vid*, *vis*   d. see

B Skills and Strategies 12: Organizing Notes in Timelines
Answer the following questions about Skills and Strategies 12. (2 points each)

1. When taking notes, a reader can use a timeline to help organize the order in which events happen in a reading. **True or False?**

2. Which of the following would you *not* look for in a reading to help you make a timeline?
   a. dates   b. numbers   c. reasons   d. sequence words

3. You should not create a timeline by writing events in a list going down the page.
   True or False?

4. Choose the correct two words to complete the sentence.
   He began studying piano _____ 2002, and _____ March 18 he will have his first solo concert.
   a. by   b. in   c. after   d. on

5. When a timeline is written across a page, the earliest event is typically on the _____.
   a. left   b. right

Reading Quiz · Units 7 and 8

Read the passage. Then answer the questions that follow.

Disaster Tourism

Most people want to relax and enjoy themselves on their vacation. They want to   1
sit on a beach, climb a mountain, or visit a famous tourist attraction. For some people,
however, a great vacation includes a disaster. They like to visit the sites of natural
disasters, where severe weather, deadly floods, or violent earthquakes have caused
death and destruction. Following the tsunami in Southeast Asia in 2004, tourists came
to see the damage, take pictures, and take home souvenirs of the disaster. Similarly,
after Hurricane Katrina in New Orleans in 2005, there were bus tours for tourists
who wanted to examine the flood damage with their own eyes. These are examples of
disaster tourism.

Why do people want to visit communities where there has been widespread damage   2
and terrible loss? Experts who study disaster tourism say there are several reasons.
First, people are naturally curious. When there is a disaster, they want to see what has
happened. However, there is a dark side to this kind of tourism. Communities that are
struggling to rebuild after a disaster often do not want these tourists.

Other tourists, however, come because they want to help. There are different ways   3
that tourists can provide assistance after a natural disaster. At these times, the number
of tourists usually goes down, which adds to the community's problems. This can
be especially difficult for communities that depend on tourism. Visiting these places
after a disaster can benefit the economy. When tourists spend money, they help the
community to rebuild. Experts give two pieces of advice to tourists who want to help
in this way. First, they should wait for a few weeks or months until the community is
ready to receive its first visitors. Second, they should use hotels and restaurants that are
owned by people in the community. That way, they can ensure their money will stay in
the community.

Another way tourists can have a positive impact on these communities is as   4
volunteers. Some experts have called this idea, *voluntourism.* Tourists come to help
rebuild homes, businesses, and schools in the disaster area. Again, experts advise
that people wait for a few weeks or months. Also, they should volunteer through an
organization that understands the community's needs.

A final reason for a visit to the site of a natural disaster is that it can provide an   5
educational opportunity. It can help tourists understand the power of nature and remind
them of the need to respect its potential for destruction.

Reading Quiz · Units 7 and 8 (continued)

A Main Idea Check

1. What is the main idea of the whole reading? (5 points)
   a. Some people like to visit the site of natural disasters on vacation.
   b. Volunteering is a popular way to spend a vacation.
   c. Natural disasters can cause terrible destruction and loss of life.

2. Match each paragraph main idea below to a paragraph from the reading. Write the number of the paragraph on the blank line. (5 points)

   _____ Spending money as a tourist can help communities in disaster areas.

   _____ Visiting the site of a natural disaster can teach tourists about the destructive power of nature.

   _____ Some people visit disaster sites because they want to see the damage.

B A Closer Look
Look back at the reading to answer the following questions. (2 points each)

1. A visit to the site of a battle in a war is an example of disaster tourism. **True or False?**

2. What kind of tourists illustrate "the dark side" of disaster tourism?
   a. People who don't want to spend money in disaster areas.
   b. People who don't want to help clean up disaster areas.
   c. People who are just curious and are not sensitive to the needs of the community.

3. Choose two items below to complete the sentence:
   Tourists help after a natural disaster by _____ and _____.
   a. staying away from the area   c. buying local products
   b. volunteering   d. staying in international hotels

4. Voluntourists' efforts are most helpful right after the disaster. **True or False?**

5. Which is *not* a reason given in the reading for disaster tourism?
   a. Education   b. Volunteering   c. Curiosity   d. Adventure

C Definitions
Find words in the reading that can complete the following definitions. (2 points each)

1. If something is _____, it is very serious and can cause a lot of damage. (*adj*) Par. 1

2. _____ are things you keep in order to remember an event or trip. (*n pl*) Par. 1

3. If you are _____, you are interested in learning about the things around you. (*adj*) Par. 2

4. To _____ is to make certain. (*v*) Par. 3

5. _____ is a possibility or ability that has not developed yet. (*n*) Par. 5

Vocabulary Quiz · Units 7 and 8

Unit 7

A The words in the box are words that you studied in Unit 7. Choose the best word to complete each sentence. You will not use all the words. (2 points each)

contact	damage	dust	explode	flood	frequent
loss	mud	outer space	tremors	vulnerable	warning

1. _____ from the typhoon cost the government $2.1 billion for recovery and repairs.

2. The entire eastern edge of Asia is _____ to earthquakes because it sits on a fault line.

3. A major earthquake is always followed by many aftershocks or _____.

4. Take off your wet shoes before coming in. I don't want any _____ on my carpet.

5. Children are fascinated by _____, and some want to become astronauts.

6. Many people think natural disasters are more _____ lately because of global warming.

7. When the tsunami struck, people sitting on the beach had no _____.

8. House fires after an earthquake are often caused by gas lines that _____.

B Circle the letter of the best word to complete each sentence. The answer is always an Academic Word List word from the unit. (2 points each)

1. The _____ use of satellites makes global communication almost instant.
   a. extinct   b. widespread   c. average   d. massive

2. Officials are working on a/an _____ to help residents prepare for disaster emergencies.
   a. sign   b. mystery   c. project   d. coast

3. Although it is impossible to know the _____ location of future earthquakes, we do know the general areas where they will occur.
   a. deadly   b. violent   c. terrible   d. precise

4. In Japan, it is _____ to keep an emergency kit ready in case of an earthquake.
   a. crucial   b. extreme   c. deadly   d. frequent

5. Sir Isaac Newton had a great _____ on the study of space and astronomy.
   a. analysis   b. pressure   c. orbit   d. impact

6. People around the world _____ relief organizations to help the tsunami victims in Thailand.
   a. blocked   b. contributed to   c. impacted   d. prepared

7. Doctors _____ the animal's organs looking for signs of disease.
   a. reduced   b. destroyed   c. analyzed   d. suggested

Vocabulary Quiz (continued)

Unit 8

A The words in the box are words that you studied in Unit 8. Choose the best word to complete each sentence. You will not use all the words. (2 points each)

apart	appear	catch up	environment	green	improve
in touch	opportunity	public	reach	risky	transformation

1. In the past, workers had no _____ to take vacations because they worked too many hours.

2. The _____ from analog to digital technology was sudden and revolutionary.

3. The hotel recycled water, used _____ technologies, and had solar panels, all to help the planet.

4. Too much tourism in the rainforests is damaging the _____.

5. The family is large and they live far apart, but they all stay _____.

6. Waiting until the very last minute to book your flight can be very _____; you may not find a seat.

7. With Skype, friends and family can be _____ but feel as if they are together.

8. Soon Facebook and Twitter will _____ even the most distant parts of the world.

B Circle the letter of the best word to complete each sentence. The answer is always an Academic Word List word from the unit. (2 points each)

1. It is usually young people who most closely follow the latest _____ in fashion and technology.
   a. attractions   b. trends   c. malls   d. factories

2. People in each _____ spend their leisure time differently.
   a. enjoyment   b. option   c. generation   d. improvement

3. Canadian and Mexican workers have a _____ number of vacation days on average.
   a. productive   b. similar   c. enjoy   d. social

4. If you need _____ with your luggage, someone should be able to help you.
   a. satisfaction   b. an employee   c. assistance   d. a volunteer

5. The government _____ a no-car area in the tourist town.
   a. earned   b. established   c. united   d. appeared

6. The Internet has _____ how people book airline flights.
   a. put off   b. fixed   c. kept   d. transformed

7. When the _____ is bad, fewer people take vacations.
   a. economy   b. concert   c. site   d. entertainment

Skills and Strategies Quiz · Units 7 and 8

Unit 7

A Skills and Strategies 13: Collocations
Answer the following questions about Skills and Strategies 13. (2 points each)

1. Which one of the following would *not* typically create a collocation?

   a. an adjective and a noun
   b. an adjective and a verb
   c. a verb and a noun

2. The more collocations you know, the quicker you should be able to read. **True or False?**

3. Which noun does *not* form a collocation with the adjective *severe*?

   a. damage   b. injuries   c. reasons   d. weather

4. A collocation is formed only by a word that goes either immediately before or after another word. **True or False?**

5. How many adjective + noun collocations are there in the following short paragraph?

   High winds during the night caused a lot of damage to the town. Some tall trees fell on top of a few cars and a couple of homes. In one place, the wind blew a roof off a house. Fortunately, because the winds happened when there were few cars on the road, there were no serious accidents. According to authorities, there is only a slight chance that the winds will return tonight.

   a. 3   b. 4   c. 5   d. 6

B Skills and Strategies 14: Organizing Notes in Outlines
Answer the following questions about Skills and Strategies 14. (2 points each)

1. Choose the best two words or phrases to complete the sentence.

   Many good readers can use _____ to help them organize their _____ when reading.

   a. notes   b. support   c. main ideas   d. outlines

2. In an outline, a system of numbers and letters is useful because _____.

   a. it makes it easy to see detailed information such as dates and numbers
   b. it shows the order in which events happened
   c. it helps you put notes on paper that does not have lines on it
   d. it shows clearly what the main ideas and their supporting details are

3. Outlines should be written using only the key words, not complete sentences. **True or False?**

4. Each section of an outline should begin with _____.

   a. the main idea of that section   c. a number
   b. an introduction   d. a complete sentence

5. It is best to put as much detail into an outline as possible. **True or False?**

Skills and Strategies Quiz (continued)

Unit 8

A Skills and Strategies 15: Phrases

Answer the following questions about Skills and Strategies 15. (2 points each for questions 1–3; 4 points for question 4)

1. A phrasal verb is always a combination of a verb and only one preposition.
   True or False?

2. Words can always come between parts of the phrasal verb. **True or False?**

3. Which of the following is *not* correct.
   a. She tried the dress on.   c. She tried on the dress.
   b. She tried it on.   d. She tried on it.

4. Match each phrasal verb with its definition.
   1. *make up*   a. appear
   2. *get in*   b. invent
   3. *figure out*   c. understand
   4. *show up*   d. arrive

B Skills and Strategies 16: Reading Quickly

Answer the following questions about Skills and Strategies 16. (2 points each)

1. You can only read quickly if the reading is familiar to you. **True or False?**

2. Reading every single word will _____.
   a. help you understand the reading better
   b. slow down your reading
   c. improve your vocabulary
   d. help you focus on the main idea of the reading

3. Following along with your finger will help you improve your reading speed.
   True or False?

4. When practicing reading quickly, it is a good idea to _____.
   a. time yourself   c. make an outline
   b. read easy material   d. take notes on the side of the page

5. Chose the correct word or phrase to complete the sentence.
   To read more quickly, focus on _____ of the reading.
   a. the first sentence   c. the middle
   b. the most important words d. each word

Quizzes Answer Key

Units 1 and 2

Reading Quiz – Units 1 and 2

A Main Idea Check
1. b   2. 3, 4, 2

B A Closer Look
1. False   3. c   5. True
2. b   4. a, c

C Definitions
1. blend   4. identical
2. stretch   5. demonstrate
3. shift

Vocabulary Quiz – Units 1 and 2

Unit 1

A
1. border   5. entrance
2. depend on   6. searched
3. fake   7. freely
4. purpose   8. examined

B
1. d   3. a   5. c   7. d
2. a   4. b   6. c

Unit 2

A
1. share   5. culture
2. successful 6. influence
3. popular   7. fit in
4. origin   8. honor

B
1. b   3. a   5. d   7. c
2. b   4. b   6. b

Skills and Strategies Quiz – Units 1 and 2

Unit 1

A
1. d, a   3. False   5. True
2. c   4. a

B
1. False   3. False   5. c
2. c   4. d

Unit 2
A
1. a, b   3. b
2. c   4. 1. c; 2. a; 3. d; 4. b
B
1. True   3. False   5. d
2. b   4. c, b

Units 3 and 4

Reading Quiz – Units 3 and 4

A Main Idea Check
1. a   2. 4, 1, 2

B A Closer Look
1. c   3. False   5. True
2. b, d   4. a

C Definitions
1. Yogurt   4. diverse
2. Spices   5. negative
3. Wages

Vocabulary Quiz – Units 3 and 4

Unit 3

A
1. convenient   5. familiar
2. percentage   6. behavior
3. worries   7. produces
4. host   8. valuable

B
1. b   3. b   5. b   7. c
2. a   4. c   6. a

Unit 4

A
1. crowded   5. separate
2. distraction 6. solution
3. decrease   7. create
4. contrast   8. encourage

B
1. b   3. a   5. d   7. c
2. c   4. a   6. b

Skills and Strategies Quiz – Units 3 and 4

Unit 3

A

1. True **3.** True **5.** a
2. d, a **4.** b

B

1. False **3.** False **5.** c
2. d **4.** c, b

Unit 4

A

1. True **3.** False
2. c **4.** 1. b; 2. d; 3. a; 4. c

B

1. c **3.** b, a **5.** c
2. False **4.** d

Units 5 and 6

Reading Quiz – Units 5 and 6

A Main Idea Check

1. c **2.** 2, 3, 1

B A Closer Look

1. b **3.** b **5.** True
2. False **4.** b, c

C Definitions

1. link **4.** Quality
2. specific **5.** bark
3. Volume

Vocabulary Quiz – Units 5 and 6

Unit 5

A

1. disturb **5.** adult
2. fall asleep **6.** essential
3. nap **7.** stress
4. adjust **8.** rapidly

B

1. d **3.** c **5.** c **7.** d
2. a **4.** a **6.** b

Unit 6

A

1. equipment **5.** record
2. collection **6.** rhythm
3. notes **7.** talent
4. the rest **8.** role

B

1. d **3.** d **5.** b **7.** d
2. a **4.** c **6.** a

Skills and Strategies Quiz – Units 5 and 6

Unit 5

A

1. b, c, a **2.** c **3.** a

B

1. False **3.** False **5.** True
2. a, b **4.** d

Unit 6

A

1. True **3.** a
2. c **4.** 1. b; 2. c; 3. a; 4. d

B

1. True **3.** False **5.** a
2. c **4.** b, d

Units 7 and 8

Reading Quiz – Units 7 and 8

A Main Idea Check

1. a **2.** 3, 5, 2

B A Closer Look

1. False **3.** b, c **5.** d
2. c **4.** False

C Definitions

1. severe **4.** ensure
2. Souvenirs **5.** Potential
3. curious

Vocabulary Quiz – Units 7 and 8

Unit 7

A

1. Damage
2. vulnerable
3. tremors
4. mud
5. outer space
6. frequent
7. warning
8. explode

B

1. b
2. c
3. d
4. a
5. d
6. b
7. c

Unit 8

A

1. opportunity
2. transformation
3. green
4. environment
5. in touch
6. risky
7. apart
8. reach

B

1. b
2. c
3. b
4. c
5. b
6. d
7. a

Skills and Strategies Quiz – Units 7 and 8

Unit 7

A

1. b
2. True
3. c
4. False
5. b

B

1. d, a
2. d
3. True
4. a
5. False

Unit 8

A

1. False
2. False
3. d
4. 1. b; 2. d; 3. c; 4. a

B

1. False
2. b
3. False
4. a
5. b